GRIEVE CREATE BELIEVE

Process Your Loss with
Intention and Truth

RACHEL GEORGE

Published in the United States
ISBN: 978-0-578-61719-0
Library of Congress Control Number: 2019919517

Cover design: Rachel George
Typesetting and graphic design: Rachel George
Photography: Rachel George
Cover and interior illustrations: Lisa Glanz, lisaglanz.com
Hymn formatting: Michael Kravchuk, michaelkravchuk.com

Dedicated with love to Clive Samuel and Winona Joy:

Knowing you and being your mama has been a great privilege.

I'd choose you again and again, even knowing the tremendous pain that would accompany the marvelous joy.

You are missed. You are loved. You are remembered.

You give me courage and so much happiness.

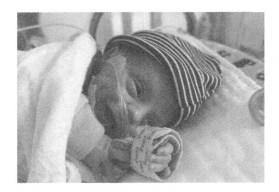

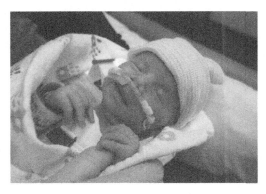

CONTENTS

Introduction..1

Chapter 1 - Lament: Permission to Grieve & Mourn................5

Chapter 2 - Peace: Protect Yourself..23

Chapter 3 - Comfort: Seek the Lord's Comfort....................43

Chapter 4 - Love: Identity as a Beloved Child of God..........71

Chapter 5 - Faith: Growing Our Trust in God......................91

Chapter 6 - Hope: Living in Hope & Awaiting Heaven........115

Chapter 7 - Grace: Freely Given & Freely Received............135

Chapter 8 - Courage: Combat Fears, Lies, & the Enemy.....159

Chapter 9 - Joy: Transformation & Renewal.......................187

Chapter 10 - Your Story: Process, Write, & Embrace Your Story.........209

Chapter 11 - Our Story: A Glimpse into God's Big Story.....221

Acknowledgements:...244

Notes:...246

Resources:..250

Dear Reader,

You've experienced a great loss. Your life is now divided into *before* and *after*, and it will never be the same. I am so sorry.

My grieving mama heart aches for you as you mourn. The loss of three children has broken and reshaped me. By God's grace, I live most days with renewed hope and even joy. My journey has not come without struggle, but within the wrestling and intentional processing I've experienced healing.

This book is for anyone who has lost a loved one and wants to process their loss with intention and the truth of scripture. These verses have been my focus as I've sought His truth:

> *Behold, you delight in truth in the inward being,*
> *and you teach me wisdom in the secret heart.*
> *Let me hear joy and gladness;*
> *let the bones that you have broken rejoice.*
> *-Psalm 51: 6, 8 (ESV)*

—

Everyone else stood, but I remained seated. I wondered at the lyrics of a popular worship song. *But would they still sing that if their worst fears were realized? Really?* My cynical heart clenched harder.

Then my gaze drifted to my friend who lost her son yet worshiped with authenticity. *What about her?* My muscles eased a bit as I watched her worship.

I saw hands raised in praise, belonging to a man with cancer—many years into his journey. *Really, still?* Unable to argue with his response, a lump formed in my throat.

My eyes finally landed on a friend pouring her heart before a God who chose not to heal her earthly body. Passionate and sincere, her voice praised her Maker wholeheartedly.

Watching God's children gave me courage to mumble along even when the words were forced. As the song continued, my voice grew stronger. Their faith challenged me and pointed me back to the Truth. I hope this book and my story can somehow do that for you. As you bear witness to my pain and honest struggle, I pray that God will draw you to Himself and give you strength.

—

After we lost our first baby through miscarriage, I silently struggled for months. Lonely and scared, I faced the first true suffering in my life and found I was ill-equipped to cope with the pain. As I'll share in later chapters, the experience of losing my sweet baby shaped me and forever changed how I handle deep wounds.

When my five-week-old son Clive died the next year, I knew better. I needed God's truth for comfort. The scriptures that fill these pages were scrawled in my journal in the months following my son's death. Many of the ideas that have evolved into these chapters were part of my early processing through grief. God was near as I sought Him. I also embraced creative avenues to help myself process. I journaled, blogged, painted, and created. I expressed my thoughts and shared. I wrestled with God and hard truths: *Is God good? Is He sovereign? Why do we suffer?* In this struggle, I found beauty and joy in creating.

Little did I know, about a year after I wrote portions of this book I'd revisit it with eyes of a newly bereaved mother yet again. My one-week-old daughter Winnie died unexpectedly only fourteen months after Clive. In unrelated circumstances, our son and daughter were ripped from our earthly lives. Numb and broken once again, it took six months to even begin to process the shock of losing her.

As I reread the words I'd written just over one year earlier, I felt betrayed. *How could I have known such hope, joy, and certainty after Clive died? And now? I don't think I'll ever feel that way again.* But I persisted. Darkness was a pit that sucked life from me, and I needed to enter the light. Seven months after Winnie died, I returned to writing. I paused when we welcomed our adopted daughter into our home, and then I revisited my manuscript again—four years after our miscarriage, three years after Clive died, and two years after Winnie died.

I wrote this book in stages as I've continued to process and learn. It's richer, fuller, and more complex than the first draft, as it's been a companion through my ever-changing road of grief and faith. The differences between Clive and Winnie's deaths deepened my understanding of the ways people process loss. I still don't understand His ways, and I may never understand this side of heaven, but I press forward.

God created us with wisdom *and* creativity. When I ignore the truth, I risk becoming lost in my own version of reality, guided by emotions and absorbed in self-expression. I might find myself repeating "I am strong enough" or on an endless search for answers within. Yet by ignoring my emotions, I risk stifling authentic healing as I conform to expectations of Christian culture. I might accept thoughts such as: "God will never give you more than you can handle." "True faith cannot be shaken." "Everything happens for a reason." Without permission to question or express anger to God, a distant-hearted faith can develop.

As I engaged both my heart and mind, I found healing. This book is a product of my grief and mourning, but not the work of someone with professional training and expertise. While it's not comprehensive enough to represent everyone's different journeys, I hope it provides you with the freedom and permission to grieve in your own way. It is my prayer that this book will encourage, challenge, and strengthen you as you navigate this road of loss.

You'll find the book organized into eleven chapters: Lament, Peace, Comfort, Love, Faith, Hope, Grace, Courage, Joy, Your Story, and Our Story. Follow whatever order you'd like, and take your time. It's okay to go slowly and be gentle with yourself. My story unfolds through the various topics in these pages, but you can read a more complete account in the last chapter.

The pages are filled with art, verses, creative responses, hymns, and reflection questions. Please read the verses within this text. I have been that person—breezing quickly through the holy word of God and onto the words written by a feeble human. But if you take anything from this book, may it be *His words.* If you write anything in your journal, may it be *His words.* If you find truth, *may it be from Him* and not from me. To Him be all the glory, honor, and power.

You might brush past the creative responses with thoughts like, "I'm not an artist," or "I'm not good at art." Creativity includes our mind, body, and soul and isn't limited to visual art. Writing poems, letters, and journaling can be creative expression, as can painting, drawing, and doodling. Spatial design or decorating can satisfy the need to express. Kinesthetic movement such as dance, yoga, walking, or other exercise can, too. Even gardening and being in nature can be creative expression. Parenting, leading, working, doing acts of service, gift-giving, and building friendship can all be examples of the way you may use creativity to heal. Making food, providing hospitality, growing spiritually, and praying are included. Don't limit your idea of creativity. Finding a creative outlet will help you as you grieve.

Finally, I encourage you to find local support at your church, a GriefShare Group (griefshare.org), or a local bereavement group. There are also many online communities that offer wonderful support on what can be a lonely journey. You can also share and connect with others by tagging your posts #grievecreatebelieve. At samandrachelgeorge.com, you'll find a list of helpful resources including books, blogs, music, and websites.

May this book be a beautiful work of art glorifying to God and pointing you to Him. May your hurts and brokenness feel seen. May we be surrounded and enveloped in His great love for us.

With love,
Rachel

CHAPTER ONE

Lament

PERMISSION TO GRIEVE AND MOURN

Permission to Grieve

Dear soul,

May you feel permission to grieve. May you feel permission to *be* where you are right now. You need not move along quickly, despite what you hear:

"Just keep yourself busy."

"Hasn't it been long enough?"

"I think it's time for you to move on"

You feel darkness and depression. And—while uncomfortable—it is okay to be broken. It is expected. You have experienced trauma and cannot expect the pain to dissipate quickly.

Repeat these words until you believe them: "It's okay not to be okay."

You're tired. You're broken. You're deeply wounded. It's okay not to be okay.

And it's okay to wait awhile before you are ready to come back to this chapter. This is your permission. Sometimes we need to pause before we're able to embrace healing. Don't let coping become your new way of life, but allow it to assist you for now. Grief is exhausting, and it might be days, weeks, months, or even years until you're ready to face it. Focus on one day and one step at a time.

Take a deep breath and give yourself permission to enter into lament and mourning when you are ready.

> *I am worn out from all my groaning.*
> *All night long I flood my bed with weeping*
> *and drench my couch with tears.*
> *My eyes grow weak with sorrow;*
> *They fail because of all my foes.*
> *-Psalm 6:6-7 (NIV)*

REFLECT: In what ways do you feel pressured by others in your grief? How can you combat the pressure to return to "normal"?

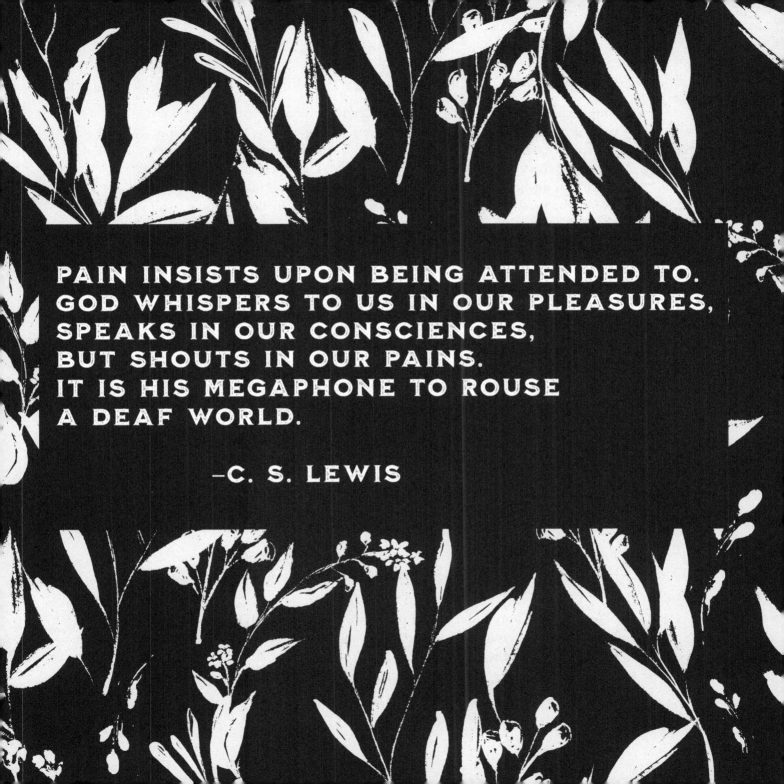

PAIN INSISTS UPON BEING ATTENDED TO.
GOD WHISPERS TO US IN OUR PLEASURES,
SPEAKS IN OUR CONSCIENCES,
BUT SHOUTS IN OUR PAINS.
IT IS HIS MEGAPHONE TO ROUSE
A DEAF WORLD.

–C. S. LEWIS

Deep Pain

I knew there would be tears and sadness, but I never anticipated the physical pain of grief. The oppressive pressure in my chest grew heavier. I curled in a heap alone on our bed and wept inconsolably—my body gasping and shaking. When the tears dried and my breathing slowed, I lay in the too-quiet room and prayed for my heart to stop. *Can't I just go join them? Can I trade myself for them?* Eventually I rose and grabbed some medicine to help me sleep, hoping to hush the screaming pain.

—

As we drove through the mountains of Washington a few weeks later, my anger grew at the peaceful view outside. Majestic mountains were peaked with snow; sunshine spilled over the tops. *How can beauty still exist in a world without my baby?* I clawed my arms red, wanting to feel the pain of Winnie's death. The physical pain mirrored the agony in my heart, but it didn't bring relief.

I turned toward my husband as he drove, angry at his silence.

"The flashbacks are back. It hurts so much, and I feel so alone." I could hardly focus on life in front of me, as tears streamed down my face, and scratches spread across my forearms.

"Me too," Sam replied.

> *My joy is gone; grief is upon me; my heart is sick within me.*
> *-Jeremiah 8:18 (ESV)*

Remember in the deep pain that you are not alone. Generations of people have suffered before you. I don't share this to diminish your sorrow, but to help you normalize these intense emotions.

You may feel: unrest and lack of peace; anger and indignation; frustration and bitterness; darkness and abandonment; exposed, abused, and cast out. You are not alone in the pain of your grief.

REFLECT: What are your physical and emotional responses to your loss? How do you cope in these moments?

Coping and Numbness

After Clive died, I threw myself into the hard work of grief: I read, I wrote, I created, I walked, I cried, and I shared. In a beautiful, exhausting, and all-consuming manner, my mothering energy poured into my grief, and the process drew me close to the memories of Clive.

But after Winnie died, I could not enter into intentional grief. Uninterested in social interactions and upset by the happy families on my newsfeed, I found myself desperate for distraction on Netflix. One night, a Japanese reality show named *Terrace House* brought unexpected comfort with its subtitles requiring me to focus and its hilarious hosts allowing me to forget my pain. Sam laughed as I began using words like *itadakimas* and *konbanwa*, and chatted about Misaki and Hikaru's budding romance. *Would they end up together?* The drama of a house full of 20-somethings in Tokyo provided the perfect diversion for a few weeks.

Sometimes we require short-term coping mechanisms. We need distractions and time-fillers because grief is exhausting. It can't be our new way of life, but it can be a temporary solution.

The pain would reemerge after the show ended and the chocolate disappeared, so I gradually turned to face it. I began the dance of grief, cautiously stepping forward in processing and then retreating back into distraction. Every part of it was healing and grief-work, but I had to find my own pace and path.

You have permission to grieve in your own way and in your own time.

Why are you cast down, O my soul,
and why are you in turmoil within me?
Hope in God; for I shall again praise him,
my salvation and my God.

-Psalm 42:5 (ESV)

REFLECT: What are your preferred coping mechanisms? How can you set limits so you do not grow dependent on coping as a way of avoiding pain?

AT MY lowest, GOD IS MY Hope.
AT MY darkest, GOD IS MY Light.
AT MY weakest, GOD IS MY Strength.
AT MY saddest GOD IS MY Comforter.
- AUTHOR UNKNOWN

Embracing Pain and Healing

Have you ever pushed through your week when you have a virus? Your body might beg for sleep, but Dayquil's more convenient. Instead of healing, it masks your symptoms so you can continue your busy life. What you need is *rest*, and the pain in your body tells you so.

In the midst of loss, you may push grief away instead of facing it. Let the pain remind you to slow down and take time to heal. Grief manifests in symptoms such as fatigue, anger, anxiety, sorrow, irritability, despair, and disinterest. View these feelings as a necessary signal to set aside time for healing.

While it's difficult, expressing your emotions will prepare your heart for healing. Acknowledging your pain is not a sign of weakness, nor is it a lack of faith. You are humble in admitting you are not okay. You are strong as you face the pain and accompanying emotions.

By recognizing your need for space to grieve, you acknowledge your pain. It's too exhausting to do all the time, but you can allow your grief to release rather than build. Suppressed grief will come out in another form—often ugly and harmful to you and those you love.

I acknowledged my pain by:

>Accepting my lack of energy and inability to do the simplest of daily routines.

>Avoiding social situations and exhausting conversations.

>Recognizing my strong emotions (anger, sadness, fatigue) related to grief, even if they came out in circumstances seemingly unrelated to grief.

—

I called Sam from my car, sobbing so heavily I could hardly speak. Less than twenty minutes earlier, I'd pulled into the Target parking lot with a confident plan. There was a return to make; I would grab a San Pellegrino and popcorn from the café; I'd peruse the store a bit; and finally, I would head to Sam's Club on some coffee shop errands.

I stepped up to the service counter. It was a nice gift, but a duplicate—no sense in keeping it. The clerk scanned the item and receipt quickly, "Okay, its back on your card."

With a brief nod, I walked away, too disappointed to make a fuss about the money credited back to the gift-giver. *Would they know I returned the gift?* I tried to shake it off. *Oh well, I didn't need the store credit, anyway.* Heading to the café for my popcorn, an "ON BREAK" sign greeted me. I turned to grab a cart and attempted a loop through the women's clothing before emotion overwhelmed me, and I ran out of the store.

Thankfully, the tears hit after I was back in the car. A full-blown panic attack followed. I could hardly breathe or think. *Was the car closing in on me?* Screaming and crying, I felt paralyzed. Eventually, my hands clamored to call Sam. Through gasping sobs, I told him I messed up on a Target return, and they didn't have popcorn. He listened patiently, even though I'm sure he didn't understand my tears. After coaching me for at least twenty minutes on the phone, he offered to make the forty-minute drive to pick me up. I pulled myself together enough to make it home, but the Sam's Club trip would have to wait.

Later, I asked my therapist Jessica what happened. *Seriously, I had a panic attack about popcorn.* Her response was helpful: "You had a plan. When things didn't go according to plan, it felt as if you lost control. Those emotions reminded you of other instances in your life when you didn't have control."

My Target popcorn plan going awry instantly triggered these emotional memories: never knowing what a day at the hospital would entail, not getting to hold Clive before emergency surgery, and going home without him.

We acknowledge our pain by recognizing our strong emotions are related to grief. My panic attack sent a flashing signal: I need to take time to process right now. Nearly a year after Clive died, I still needed to provide space and an outlet for my grief. The pain hurts, but ignoring it didn't make it go away.

REFLECT: How might you feel tempted to mask your emotions, numb the pain, or release them unhealthily? How can you provide space to grieve?

Rescue me
from my enemies,
LORD,
for I hide myself
IN YOU.
- PSALM 143:9 -

Learning to Lament

In the Bible, the Psalms are full of lament and honest grief. These feelings are not masked or pushed aside. God can handle our difficult thoughts, questions, and emotions. The examples in the Psalms are an outward expression of lament and mourning. It is important to have times of quiet reflection of your inward grief but also valuable to express your mourning to others.

> How long, LORD? Will you forget me forever?
> How long will you hide your face from me?
> How long must I wrestle with my thoughts
> and day after day have sorrow in my heart?
> How long will my enemy triumph over me?
> -Psalm 13:1-2 (NIV)

Lament is beautiful. It's raw and human, spanning generations and cultures and connecting us to one another.

Lament is exhausting. You don't have a capacity to do this and only this. At times, you may look normal as you go to work and run errands. Your face may not be tear-streaked, and you might even smile. There's a time and place for both.

Lament is honest. The Psalms are full of painful, beautiful laments. These verses contain both orienting and disorienting passages. As we read, we often see that in the process of writing and lamenting, the Psalmist reorients toward God. The honesty and communication with God, even in the midst of feeling abandoned and disoriented, draw the psalmist back to trust.[2] In my own journey, a prayer or vulnerable conversation often starts as a lament and ends with reorientation to the truth.

Lament is unexpectedly hopeful. Most of the lamenting Psalms end with a hope and trust in the Lord, despite a lack of understanding. Grief isn't tidy. It's non-linear and nonsensical. As we lament our losses and admit our disorientation, God has an opportunity to enter and draw us toward Himself.

In my early days of grief, I longed to live in a society that donned black clothes to express their mourning. On a trip to Thailand in 2016, Thai culture's collective grief after the death of King Bhumibo was on full display. Portraits of the King were everywhere I turned, adorned with flowers. Even two months after he passed, streets were full of people wearing black in mourning. It was beautiful to see their shared grief, to bear witness to their common suffering.

While our culture doesn't have an outward symbol, I chose to share my heart through my writing—to lament the deaths of my children outwardly. By balancing *inward grief* and *outward mourning*, I expressed feelings and processed through pain. Drawing loved ones into my suffering, my writing equipped them to support and care for me.

Vulnerability is not weakness. While not everyone will choose to share their pain, processing, and lamentations publicly, it's freeing to share with even one or two confidants. It removes the shame we carry in grief when we open up about the hurt. By giving words to our deepest feelings, we can unexpectedly bless those around us as it leads them to process pain in their own lives.

Allow me to give you permission to lament. Here are some treasured words from friends after Winnie's death:

"It seemed like all those sympathy cards had all of grief figured out. But my initial thoughts of you both was that you were departing into an unknown place of grief. I would never want to brush off the deep grief you all are feeling with some sort of canned optimism. I am lamenting with you. I'm sorry that this is the pilgrimage thrust upon you. It is exceedingly difficult. My prayer as I approach Jesus with puzzled reverence is that He would redeem in the way that He does."

"I also pray that well-meaning people will not try to cheer you up or try to pull you out of where you are—may you continue to grieve, as I believe it keeps us connected to heaven and our eyes set on our real home."

REFLECT: List some practical ways you can outwardly mourn and privately grieve. How can you provide time for these actions? What holds you back from lamenting?

Give sorrow words.
The grief that does not speak
whispers the o'er-fraught heart,
and bids it break.

—*William Shakespeare*

A God Who Knows and Cares

My head was pounding, but I reached over to turn up the volume again—hoping the noise would force me to forget. With my eyes fixed beyond my white knuckles, the car plowed ahead. On an overpass, I considered jerking the wheel sharply to the right. *But what if I survived? Wouldn't that be worse? And what about Sam?*

Long drives often provided a time for reflection and quiet tears, but lately they were replaced with an angry urge to drive away and never return.

Our miscarriage came at an unstable time in our lives. Darkness overwhelmed me. I felt alone, numb, and bitter. Unwilling to receive the Lord's comfort and allowing myself to be filled with rage, I pushed Him away. *Is this urge to numb the pain why people turn to addictions? How can I keep living this way?* A wall went up, and I struggled, utterly alone, for months.

God gently continued to seek me with His still, small voice of truth and love. I compared myself with others who had been through hardships, embarrassed by my weak faith. It was as though I didn't even have the strength to depend on His strength. But His love is steadfast, and He was still there, months later, when I was finally ready to talk and receive His comfort. He worked in my hard heart, and He revealed His love and grace for me.

> *Truly my soul finds rest in God;*
> *my salvation comes from him.*
> *Truly he is my rock and my salvation;*
> *he is my fortress, I will never be shaken.*
> *Trust him at all times, you people;*
> *pour out your hearts to him, for God is our refuge.*
> *-Psalm 62:1, 8 (NIV)*

In the midst of your pain, dear reader, may you seek the Lord. He knows your pain and enters into your suffering. He is a God with wounds, a God who understands. We see this in Jesus' preparation for suffering and death. In the Garden of Gethsemane, He pleads with God to take the cup and was in anguish, sweating blood (Luke 22:42-44). He cried out, forsaken. He was bruised, pierced, mocked, crucified and abandoned, while His Father knew the pain of watching.

The enemy pursues me,
he crushes me to the ground;
he makes me dwell in darkness
like those long dead.
So my spirit grows faint within me;
my heart within me is dismayed.
Let the morning bring me word of your unfailing love,
for I have put my trust in you.
Show me the way I should go,
for to you I entrust my life.
Rescue me from my enemies, LORD,
for I hide myself in you.
-Psalm 143:3-4; 8-9 (NIV)

After Winnie died, I struggled to feel the presence of God. For months a sense of abandonment prevailed. *Why is there such an uncomfortable silence?* I was left confused by the God who had been so comforting and *near* to me after Clive died. *Has He forgotten me?* The scriptures promise us He does not abandon us, but I *felt* as though He had. A friend gave me a beautiful image as she described God's silence. She pictured me weeping alone in a bedroom, and Jesus sitting in a chair next to the bed weeping with me. *What could He have said that would have comforted me?* Perhaps there were no words.

You may not always feel God's presence, but you can hold on to the promise "He will never leave you" (Deuteronomy 31: 6). He has not abandoned us. Ever-patient, He does not expect us to rush along in our lamentations.

REFLECT: Did your loved one experience pain? Allow yourself to reflect on the understanding Jesus has of deep pain. Allow yourself to reflect on the complete healing and restoration that Christ offers in life with Him in heaven.

O Love That Wilt Not Let Me Go

George Mathenson   Albert L. Peace

Creative Response:

Read a Psalm a day. When you don't know where else to turn in the Bible, these are passages that resonate deeply with feelings of suffering and pain. When you find passages that speak to you, write the laments and/or praises in your journal. May they be a continual reminder of God's love for you amidst the pain. Some of my favorite Psalms of lament include: Psalms 6, 13, 42, 55, 77, 89, and 142.

Write your own lament. What are the deepest moments of pain in your life? Write a lament about them, embracing your honest feelings. Let your emotions be expressed freely to God in words. Complete sentences aren't necessary, just write a few words if that's all you can manage. Express your anger, sorrow, confusion, abandonment, hope, joy, fear, or peace. Read it aloud. Cry it out.

Paint your pain. With art, you can create something that words cannot express. Use any type of paint to express your emotions. Use paper, a scrap board, or canvas. Consider the use of different colors or shades to convey your emotions. Use a variety of brushes, combs, or layering to add texture. You can glue fabric scraps and paint on top of those for extra dimension, too. While you may not have a vision for the end product, the process itself will be healing. Consider using this as a backdrop to paint layers on as you go through this book.

Get moving. Sometimes our body needs a physical response to the emotions we are experiencing. Whether it's pounding it out in a run or just getting outside for a walk, let some of your emotions release physically. Allowing this to become part of your routine will help create a positive outlet for your emotions and may protect from harmful habits.

Room for lament. I remember a few friends telling me what they did when they heard of Winnie's sudden death. Pulling over and weeping behind the steering wheel. Driving to their small group leader's house to cry and pray. I hadn't considered the impact others experienced on that dark day. But yet—weeping, deep sorrow, lament. Perhaps it would be helpful to ask others to share their deep lament with you. It might be something they won't share without your request. Make room to listen to others' expressions of grief and guide them in listening to your own expression.

Journal and reflect on your progress, amid setbacks. Regular journaling can help you reflect on the progress you've made in your grief journey, see patterns, and remind you of the moments of clarity and truth shining through. Some people find that the processing and releasing of thoughts through writing helps allow them to sleep or rest better.

Create an art journal. Besides a journal for writing out thoughts, prayers, verses, and memories, I encourage you to start an art journal. The best kind of material for this would be a larger sized sketchbook with heavy paper. You can organize your artwork for this book in there, or you could create your own art journal on heavyweight paper and use string, rings, or a binder to group it together. For your first art journal project, focus on the word "pain". Use collage elements from newspapers, magazines, old books, scraps of paper, or images printed from the internet to create a page focused on pain. Consider the colors and words that represent pain in your life. Include a verse, part of a song, or some phrases from the lament you wrote.

Find and create an Ebenezer Stone. The Ebenezer stone is mentioned in 1 Samuel 7:12: "Then Samuel took a stone and set it up between Mizpah and Shen and called its name Ebenezer; for he said, "Till now the LORD has helped us." The name Ebenezer means "stone of help," and this stone stood as a powerful physical reminder of God's sovereignty, power, and faithfulness as the Israelites defeated the Philistines and took back the Ark of the Covenant.[5] Building a collection of Ebenezer Stones can provide a physical reminder to you of God's help and deliverance. Look for your first stone today and label it with a paint marker. You can use a simple word, such as "lament," a phrase, or anything meaningful at this point in your process. Put it in a spot that will serve to remind you of God's presence.

What can you do in the moments of deepest pain? Cry. Pray. Groan (the Spirit intercedes for you). Sleep. Vent to God. Pour your heart out to a trusted friend. Look in the mirror and tell yourself the Truth. Write it out. Just allow yourself to feel.

Five Minute Activity: Stream of Consciousness Journaling. Allow yourself to use "stream of consciousness" writing, in which you write your free-flowing thoughts without taking time to stop, edit, or censor them. This is a great tool for managing big emotions and discovering underlying feelings.

CHAPTER TWO

Peace

PROTECT YOURSELF

Where is the Peace?

I endured a lengthy hospital stay and a major surgery to bring Clive into the world. I watched as my sick child suffered and died. The week of the funeral and services passed with numbness as our family honored Clive. And then a stomach virus hit both Sam and me immediately after the burial. We lay on the couch for days, our physical sickness intensifying our deep sadness. I found myself too weak to distract from my pain; there was nothing else to plan, nothing to rally around, no prayer requests to send, and no updates to give.

Family headed home. I collapsed, realizing my capacity had dramatically changed.

After the death of my child, it felt as though the world stopped spinning, yet I looked around and saw life continued for everyone else. I wandered around the grocery store: numb, tired, and lost. I desired a physical change indicating I wasn't the same person—and Brittany Spear's infamous head shaving didn't seem all that ridiculous anymore. I wanted to scream at people, "MY CHILD DIED!" Everything I did was emotionally, physically, and mentally exhausting.

In the midst of all-consuming fatigue, it became important to find and protect my peace.

In a culture that puts so much emphasis on work, productivity, and efficiency, it's hard to find moments of outward peace—even after loss, when we should give ourselves the most grace. But it's critical—and biblical. In the Old Testament, Sabbath laws allowed for rest and worship, while in the New Testament, Jesus withdrew to quiet places for respite and reconnection with the Father.

As a teacher, I was on summer break for almost two months after our son passed away. I slept, regrouped, and worked through trauma. My husband, however, returned to work less than a week after the funeral. Spreadsheets, meetings, emails—he couldn't care less about any of it. Every day he returned home drained and defeated.

We set boundaries for ourselves and for others by learning to say no, guard our family time, and ask for help. We learned to accept the generosity of friends and family when they brought meals and helped in other ways. Sometimes, we *wanted* to do more but had to draw a clear line on our limitations—even for enjoyable things. We were exhausted *all the time*.

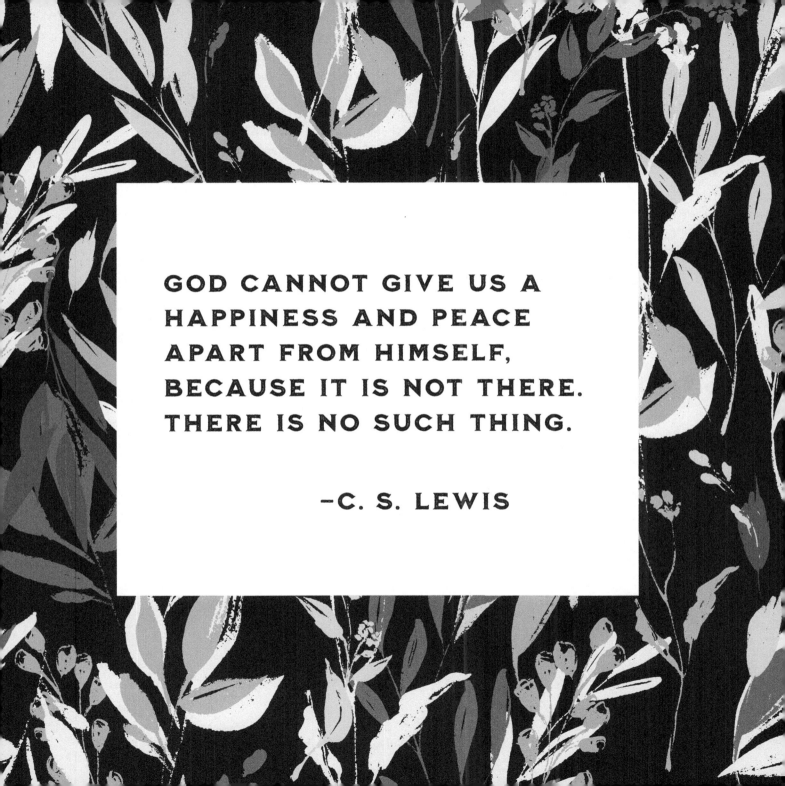

GOD CANNOT GIVE US A
HAPPINESS AND PEACE
APART FROM HIMSELF,
BECAUSE IT IS NOT THERE.
THERE IS NO SUCH THING.

-C. S. LEWIS

Sometimes, we made mistakes—like gutting and remodeling our kitchen six months after Clive died. We thought we had more energy and capacity than we did, and our bodies, spirits, and marriage suffered as a result. We've learned that even after a year or two, as life begins its "new normal", it is important to guard and protect our time and peace. There are still days of complete exhaustion, and all signs point to grief.

—

God gives us a promise of rescuing, sustaining, and carrying us through the most troubling waters. He is the source of peace, and we cannot have it apart from Him. Continue to draw near to Him. Create boundaries to have outward peace in your life, but do not neglect time with God to give you the true peace you need.

> *Even to your old age and gray hairs*
> *I am he, I am he who will sustain you.*
> *I have made you and I will carry you;*
> *I will sustain you and I will rescue you.*
> *-Isaiah 46:4 (NIV)*

REFLECT: What boundaries do you need to set to protect your peace?

Protect Your Peace

Winnie's death left me exposed. Our broken hearts were on display; our tragedy felt all too visible—full of gawking, questions, and pitying looks. Even kindness and compassion began to feel like an invasion of privacy.

A few months later, we built a fence around our backyard. As we dug and sunk posts, the fence became more than another project. While we mixed cement, the literal hedge of protection reminded us of our need for emotional and relational boundaries. As we hammered side-by-side, we reclaimed a small plot of privacy and peace.

We bounced back and forth—and still do—in our capacity for social interactions, church involvement, work commitments, home projects, and time with family. We'd increase involvement, overdo it, and retreat. We regularly talked about ways we could protect our peace or create peace in our lives—and we regularly made mistakes. While there is nothing we could do to change the past or undo the trauma we experienced, we could establish guardrails around our life in little ways to prevent it from spiraling out of control.

What does protecting your peace look like? It's different for everyone, but here are some simple and practical things you can do:

Set boundaries with your schedule. Practice saying no (without feeling guilty). You may need to scale back at work, at church, or at home. Take time to think through your commitments and set some boundaries—even if only temporarily.

Take a special trip. Within a month of each of our children's funerals, Sam and I got away to a quiet place for some time to rest and recharge. The mountains of Asheville, North Carolina and the solitude of Mayne Island, British Columbia welcomed us with rest. While it was far from a "fun" vacation, it provided special time together. It was necessary to take some time for this when so many things around us had returned to 'normal'. Even if you can't get far away, consider smaller ways you can unplug from responsibilities and rest.

Guard your family time. We were busy and emotionally exhausted during the workweek but took time on the weekends to reconnect, process, and talk about how we were doing. It was easy to be self-focused in our grief, but we tried to take time to listen, understand, and love each other.

Guard your time with God. While it is hard, it's a critical time to draw near to Him with consistency. Even when you do not feel His presence, God is there. Pour out your laments. You may find—like me—you need longer segments of time to enter into spiritual moments. As you look for something to fill the void in your life, turn your eyes to Him—the Suffering Servant and Loving King—who can handle all your questions, thoughts, and emotions.

Ask for help. Many people will offer to help and would consider it a blessing to serve you. Take time to stop and think about what needs to be done. Keep a list of practical and specific things they can do to help you: cleaning, errands, babysitting, cooking, etc.

Plan simple tasks. For months, grocery shopping exhausted me, and it was the only thing I could do that day. Doctor's appointments or time with friends was even worse. Take some time to plan errands like this in advance. Make a list, psych yourself up, and reward yourself with some rest after you're done. There is no reason to feel foolish for being exhausted after a seemingly simple task.

Practice self-care. Focus on the necessities: eat, sleep, and move. Feed yourself nutritious food, get outside, be active, and get adequate sleep. It's easy to put yourself last, especially if you have a family depending on you. Try to schedule moments of solitude and self-care. It might be small moments throughout the week, but take time to care for your body, provide nourishment, and try to reduce stress. Perhaps you can play music, practice deep breaths, go for a walk, or take an unhurried shower.

Slow down. Take time to focus on methodically doing things. It will be less stressful, and you'll be able to focus on each task as it comes. Consider simple ways you can concentrate on the present moment, such as chopping vegetables, doing five minutes of stretching, or sitting to drink a cup of tea.

Reevaluate and recognize your own capacity. Others, including those in your own family, may have different capacities and needs than you. You may need extra space and time away from the busyness of life, church and social involvement, and optional obligations. If you can't reach an agreement on how involved and busy you should be together, you may have to do things separately for a while and extend grace to one another about your differences.

Prepare to answer the hard questions that might come your way. They may come from strangers asking about your family size or pregnancy. They may come from well-meaning friends asking details or not taking care in their words. It helped me to be prepared to answer the question "How many kids do you have?" There isn't a right or wrong way to approach it, and it's okay to refrain from telling everyone if it feels too intimate to share about your child, spouse, or another loved one who has passed. It is easier with time, but it remains hard to anticipate people's reactions and to know how to move the conversation forward afterwards. A few examples of what I might say, depending on the situation:

"I have one child at home right now."

"This is my first."

"I have a son who would be three, a daughter who would be two, and a one-year-old. They are all blessings!"

"My son and daughter died as newborns, but we were blessed with our time with them."

A quick answer and replying with a question for them is always helpful to steer the conversation forwards. I often find myself trying to smooth over the rough question by mentioning the blessing that Clive and Winnie were (and are) in our lives. You are under no obligation to answer prying questions about your private life. While these are the things of everyday conversations to most, they are intimate questions concerning trauma and pain to you.

Consider and control your peace. It can be so easy to blame our lack of peace on other people or on situations. While some things are out of our control, there are some ways we can exert control. Instead of being frustrated that you have no time to rest, consider the little things you can do. Ask for help, set boundaries, find small moments of peace, take time to know your needs, and communicate them. Blaming others for your lack of peace will not help you—I can speak from experience.

Surrender your role. Sometimes you must realize that life can and will go on without you being intricately involved in everything around you. Surrender that control. See how God uses other people to fill the roles you thought only you could fill.

Give yourself grace. I missed appointments. I stamped a whole stack of letters with the postage stamp in the wrong corner. I wandered. I forgot names. Even years out, I feel like my brain is functioning at a much lower capacity. I'm slower; I'm more easily fatigued; I lose my words. This is my brain on trauma. Give yourself the grace you need for the mistakes you have and will make. As a sweet friend wrote in a card to us after Clive died, "Give yourselves the patience you'd give your newborn son."

> *I lift my eyes up to the mountains—*
> *where does my help come from?*
> *My help comes from the LORD,*
> *the Maker of heaven and earth.*
> *He will not let your foot slip—*
> *he who watches over you will not slumber.*
> *-Psalm 121:1-3 (NIV)*

REFLECT: What are some restorative things you can do? How can you take action to protect your peace today?

Build a little fence of trust
　　　Around today;
Fill the space with loving work
　　　And therein stay.
Look not through the protective rails
　　　Upon tomorrow;
God will help you bear what comes
　　　Of joy or sorrow.
　　　　　　　—Mary F. Butts

Jesus' Example of Retreating

Frantic people surround us—rushed, exhausted, distracted. Perhaps you feel the pressure, too. There's never enough time, energy, or money. We live in a world of scarcity and striving. But we weren't created to live this way, and we cannot sustain it for long seasons.

We're so governed by timetables we lose sight of the very maker and keeper of time. Even Jesus needed respite from His busy ministry, and He sought solitude and silence. He withdrew to connect with the Father.

Very early in the morning, while it was still dark, Jesus got up, left the house and went off to a solitary place, where he prayed.
-Mark 1:35 (NIV)

Then, because so many people were coming and going that they did not even have a chance to eat, he said to them,
"Come with me by yourselves to a quiet place and get some rest."
-Mark 6:31 (NIV)

At daybreak Jesus went out to a solitary place.
-Luke 4:42 (NIV)

But Jesus often withdrew to lonely places and prayed.
-Luke 5:16 (NIV)

One of those days Jesus went out to a mountainside to pray, and spent the night praying to God.
-Luke 6:12 (NIV)

Jesus, knowing that they intended to come and make him king by force, withdrew again to a mountain by himself.
-John 6:15 (NIV)

There's rhythm in these repeating words: early, withdrew, solitary, left, quiet, rest, lonely, prayed. There's wisdom in His example. It required

Peace
I LEAVE WITH YOU;
my peace
I GIVE YOU.
- JOHN 14:27 -

intentionality—even for the Son of God—but rest is necessary to our soul.

After hearing of John the Baptist's death, Jesus "withdrew by boat privately to a solitary place" (Matthew 14:13). He retreated to grieve His friend and cousin. Perhaps He wept and prayed as He traveled by boat, expecting solitude and solace when He neared the shore. But a crowd met Him, having heard of His miracles and teaching. The crowd, however friendly, was demanding attention from Him. Setting aside His rest, Jesus "had compassion on them and healed their sick" (Matthew 14:14). He fed over five thousand people that day through a miracle of loaves and fish. When the crowd was finally dismissed in the evening, He withdrew again to the mountainside to be alone. He persisted to allow this time to be possible. When work arose, He faithfully took action. However, He held space for rest, prayer, retreat, and solitude.

God heals and reveals when we remove ourselves from busyness and seek peace. In John 4:27, Jesus says, "Peace I leave with you; my peace I give you. I do not give to you as the world gives." His peace is different. May you follow the Lord's example of rest. Go to the One who takes our burdens upon Himself. Be unhurried with Jesus; rediscover rest.

REFLECT: What do you notice and admire about Jesus's times alone?

Triggers and Trauma

One of my kindergarteners reached for me as we passed through the long hallway out of the school. My breathing became strained at the squeeze of a child's tender hand. Rows of buses stood before us, but I was in the hospital room with Clive's fingers wrapped around mine—memories of my son overwhelmed my senses. My head spun as we continued walking towards the buses spewing exhaust into the air. An invisible remote pressed *mute* on the cheerful chatter around me. I led the student to the bus and slowly walked back inside the school, finally sinking into my chair and staring at my blank computer screen.

After trauma or loss, you may experience triggers and flashbacks that overwhelm your senses. You're left unable to function—straining for breath, trembling, shaking, and sweating. It's okay to feel this way—although painful, it's normal. In the moments of complete anxiety, focus your breathing and pray for peace. While there is no way to entirely prevent them, it may be helpful to try to process through triggers with a trusted friend or counselor. Consider why the event triggered a flashback for you—perhaps a smell, a place, a person, a topic of conversation—and what you could do to process through the pain, even though there's not always an answer.

Early in loss, you might be unable to remember things aside from the trauma. The final, painful moments come to mind first. Try to focus on happy memories as you rework your memories. If you lost an infant, you may recall the happiness surrounding your pregnancy and the places you went while you carried your child. If you have pictures, look at them to remind yourself of your loved one's blessed life, however short it was. With time, many of the most painful memories and triggers can become less powerful and debilitating if you are able to focus your thoughts on more positive memories.

You may find certain places trigger your emotions too. I desperately desired restorative peace when I walked in the doors to my church, but despite our community's support, it was a painfully vulnerable place. Standing to worship God felt too intimate; my soul was raw and bare. I felt anger towards God and did not want to be there surrounded by babies and happy families. *Is everyone watching me?* In an effort to avoid pity or small talk, I left a few minutes early or saddled myself next to a safe person to talk with until the church emptied.

Some weeks I couldn't even go. Over time, and with a consistent effort to remain connected to our faith community, church once again became a restorative and peaceful place.

Although I don't agree with the phrase "time heals all wounds" there *is* a healing work that happens over time if we allow ourselves to press into healing. We have to give ourselves the grace to take some time off from normal activities, entering back into them as we feel ready. Without these breaks, we don't allow time to do its work. Without intentional processing through our triggers and trauma, we don't allow ourselves the opportunity to embrace healing, despite how much time may pass. Both time and intentionality are necessary to our grief journeys.

> *You will keep in perfect peace*
> *those whose minds are steadfast,*
> *because they trust in you.*
> *-Isaiah 26:3 (NIV)*

REFLECT: What are some triggers you experience? How can you combat these triggers in a healthy way? Where is a difficult place for you to be right now? If this is a place you need to go, can you think of any action steps that will make it better?

My Hope Is Built on Nothing Less

Edward Mote

John B. Dykes

Chasing Peace and Comforts

The sun rested on our shoulders as our longboat floated through the calm waters of the Andaman Sea. Beautiful limestone formations—called karsts—rose from turquoise water. Soft white sand graced the small shore.

"That one is called James Bond Island. It's where they filmed *The Man with the Golden Gun*." The local guide paddled around the rock structures, under caverns, and took photos of us as if we were honeymooners. We'd found paradise in the waters of Thailand. Yet, throughout the entire day, I was plagued by flashbacks of Winnie's death—a mere four months earlier. My mind couldn't leave the hospital room. On the other side of the world, as far away as humanly possible, my pain and trauma remained inescapable.

> *Peace I leave with you; my peace I give to you.*
> *I do not give to you as the world gives.*
> *-John 14:27 (NIV)*

Take a moment to picture the most peaceful and comforting place you can envision. You might imagine a restful retreat, a mountain cabin, or a nap in a hammock on the beach. It's easy for us to believe there is a tangible peace we can find or create. While this is true to an extent, we fall prey to this illusion far too often. It's easy imagining life would be better if we could only have that vacation, pampering, or new comfort. We chase dreams without realizing true peace comes from soul peace. True rest comes from soul rest.

Many things in this world will not provide enduring satisfaction or rest. Peace that God gives is "not as the world gives." He gives us lasting peace that takes root in our souls. C. S. Lewis wrote in *Mere Christianity*, "Comfort is the one thing you cannot get by looking for it. If you look for truth, you may find comfort in the end. If you look for comfort, you will not get either comfort or truth — only soft soap and wishful thinking to begin with and, in the end, despair."[1] As you seek physical, emotional, and spiritual peace in your life, remember that it can only truly come from the Lord.

REFLECT: How are you tempted to chase physical comforts? What might help you focus on spiritual comfort that comes only from God?

Creative Response:

Create a peaceful place in your home. It could be a room or just a corner of your home. Maybe it is a place that reminds you of your loved one, or perhaps it is just a place of comfort. Consider what you might bring to this space that may make it more peaceful: books, a journal, plants, artwork, a blanket, a comfy chair, photos, art supplies. For some, this space might be the bedroom of their loved one. Clive's nursery became a peaceful space for me; I finished decorating it and used as a space to meet with God and process through my loss. I've known other people who have changed their child's bedroom into an art studio or peace room. Still others have found it too hard to enter their loved one's space and have created a peaceful area in a different place in the house or yard. No matter where, find a space you can fill with things that give comfort and bring joy.

Find time for silence and peace. Take a step back from the world full of noise and activity. Seek healing by allowing yourself to sit and think, silently listening to God. Journal thoughts as they pop into your head during these times of solitude.

Carve out time for creating. Set aside this time to work through prompts or activities in this book, write, or just sit and think it's easy to stay busy, but allowing purposeful time for this will help you work through your grief and emotions. It was helpful to me to have some basic supplies in a bag that I could take out and put away with ease, rather than rummaging through my boxes of art supplies. I kept it simple: my journal, art journal, colored pencils, a glue stick, pens, a coloring book, and a small pack of patterned paper. When I'm ready to create, all I have to do is grab my bag—removing the overwhelming task of gathering supplies and cleaning up a huge mess.

Art Journal Activity: Exploring the Range of Emotions. Stamp, type or write feelings that you have been experiencing. Use ripped paper (from magazines, old books, scraps, or scrapbook paper) to create a background image for the range of emotions you are feeling. Perhaps they feel like a mountain, a ball, or a wave. Maybe they feel like a storm, a broken heart, a valley, a vacuum, or black hole. Or perhaps they feel like a mess. Consider the use of colors or textures in the paper to capture some of your emotions. Decoupage or glue them into your journal, then add the feeling words you stamped or wrote. Think about these emotions and remember that they are valid and normal. Taking time to acknowledge them, pray through them, and process them will help you grow in handling your emotions in an increasingly healthy manner.

Art Journal Activity: Paint, draw, or use mixed media to create an image or symbol of the word *peace* and what it means to you right now. Does it bring to mind inner or outer peace? What colors come to mind? What symbols do you envision?

Write out your triggers. While this is an emotionally exhaustive activity, it is helpful to list some triggers you've experienced or that you anticipate experiencing—smells, places, people, doing something for the first time. After listing the trigger, write ways you could avoid, handle, or embrace it. Some cannot be avoided, but consider ways you can cope with the situation. For me, coping often involved hyper-focusing on something else at the moment, such as my hands, my breath, or a distraction on my phone. In moments of intense panic or hysteria (especially while at work or in a public setting), I often had to try to self-calm by focusing on the next small task in front of me and coaching myself through the next few minutes of that task.

Make bath salts and take a relaxing bath. Simple recipe: 1 cup Epsom salts, ¼ cup baking soda, ¼ cup sea salt, 8-10 drops of an essential oil. Essential oils can have wonderful aromas and effects. Lavender is relaxing, peppermint is invigorating, and lemon is refreshing. Find a favorite, blend them together, or just use a squirt of great-smelling body wash if you prefer. Baths provided necessary relief to me after Winnie died. On days I found all other comforts or distractions unappealing, the warm water embraced and calmed me.

Find and create your next Ebenezer Stone. As I mentioned in the first chapter, building a collection of Ebenezer Stones can provide a physical reminder to you of God's help and deliverance. Look for your next stone today and label it with a paint marker. You can use a simple word, such as "peace," a phrase, or anything meaningful at this point in your process. Put it in a spot that will serve to remind you of God's presence and help.

Create an action plan to help your recovery. Write out a list of activities that can help your recovery. Write three columns: today, this week, and this month.

Write a list of a few simple things you could do to take care of yourself in each of these sections. It can be so simple: drink water, sit and have a coffee, go for a walk, schedule counseling, talk with a friend, write in my journal for 10 minutes.

Write a letter or email to your family or coworkers. Explain to them what they can do to be helpful. Share some of your current feelings.[5]

Some examples of words you might use:

> *You can talk with me and let me know you care.*
> *Don't say "I know how you feel." Instead, say "I am sorry for your loss."*
> *Don't assume men cope with trauma better than women.*
> *Here is a list of some specific ways you can help.*
> *Don't tell me everything will be okay, but tell me you will be there.*
> *Don't try to find the reasons or explanations for why things happened—or try to explain things away with spiritual reasons. Sometimes just being there is enough.*
> *Allow some privacy and time, and don't become upset if I don't have the energy to respond.*
> *Try not to take the things I say or do too personally.*
> *Please continue to text me, call me, and invite me to things.*

Example of ours can be found on our blog:

samandrachelgeorge.com/2019/12/13/grief-letter/

Five Minute Activity: Calming shower. Turn up some music and take a shower. The music and the sensory input from the shower will have a calming effect on you. For many people, a shower feels like a safe place to cry, scream, and express big emotions.

CHAPTER THREE

Comfort

SEEK THE LORD'S COMFORT

Comfort from the Lord

In the sterile walls of Room 423, I tried to make sense of it all. My son's life was fading, but God's presence was overwhelming. In true "Jesus, take the wheel" form, I had no power of my own to pray and petition.

"I don't even have strength left to trust Him," I told my pastor. "All I can do is passively surrender."

"That's not a bad thing," he replied.

With no tasks to do and no strength to struggle, my inability loomed large. Eight weeks into our hospital stay, I stood helplessly next to Clive's bed and held his tiny hand. Surrounded by beeping monitors and pumps, I leaned *deeper still* into His presence. As all else faded away, I fell into total dependence on Him.

> *From My Journal: June 8, 2015—Two days after Clive died*
>
> Clive went to be with Jesus two days ago. Many people have spoken out about our strength through this. The reality is that we had none. It was all Him. It was far easier to trust Him than to trust ourselves. Depending on Him felt to be the easier, more peaceful, more passive thing, in the midst of such turmoil.

In contrast to the complete darkness of my miscarriage, God was my comforter and my perfect peace in the wake of Clive's death. There were—and still are—moments of frustration, doubt, and anger, but my heart did not enter the pit of despair I experienced the previous year. I knew remaining in the darkness and avoiding His comfort was futile. I *allowed* Him to be my strength instead of stubbornly trying to get through it alone. It was an act of submission—an admission of my lack of control.

Embracing God's comfort didn't come easily, but as I wrestled with pain and emptiness, I realized it is the only true comfort the world has to offer. It is lasting, real, and available, and it comes from a God who knows and cares for us intimately.

He is a God who understands. There are examples throughout the Bible of God's understanding of sorrow and of His own heartbreak. God the Father knows the anguish of His son dying—in a terrible manner—while taking on the burden of the sin of the world.

He is a God who grieves. As Jesus came to Mary and Martha after the death of Lazarus (John 11), He was deeply moved, greatly troubled, and *He wept*. With the foreknowledge that healing was coming, He entered into their grief and showed His compassion for His people. How powerful to know we serve a God who suffered and grieved.

He is a God who desires to comfort. In John 14:16, He promises to send us a comforter, the Holy Spirit, to be with us and dwell in us. In the most challenging moments, the Spirit "intercedes for us with groans that words cannot express" (Romans 8:26).

May your mourning draw you near to His arms as He quenches your parched soul. The blessing is not in the loss but in the nearness to God that we get to experience through pain and suffering.

> *Yet, I am always with you;*
> *you hold me by my right hand.*
> *You guide me with your counsel,*
> *and afterward you will take me into glory.*
> *Whom have I in heaven but you?*
> *And earth has nothing I desire besides you.*
> *My flesh and my heart may fail,*
> *but God is the strength of my heart*
> *and my portion forever.*
> *-Psalm 73:23-26 (NIV)*

REFLECT: Write out your honest feelings to the Lord. Are you able to draw near to Him for comfort? What may be getting in the way?

Blessed in the Brokenness

Sometimes God can feel especially close and comforting after loss, as He did after our son Clive died. I shared the following blog post during my pregnancy with Winnie. Re-reading it surprises me. I'm shocked at my faith and words, but I realize they are God-given because I couldn't have penned them on my own. I don't always feel full of faith, but I am grateful for the times I am. As I read them, my heart becomes re-oriented by my own words.

Blog Post: July 13, 2016—Pregnant with Winnie

I've shared before that there is such a beauty in the place of brokenness and surrender. When I have—or rather perceive to have—control over life, there is less need for dependence upon Christ for daily sustenance. In the beatitudes, Jesus says:

> *"Blessed are the poor in spirit,*
> *for theirs is the kingdom of heaven.*
> *Blessed are those who mourn,*
> *for they will be comforted."*
> *-Matthew 5:3-4 (NIV)*

I remember reading and journaling about these verses last summer after Clive died.

> *June 21, 2015: It just makes sense, this blessing. In the midst of the greatest grief, I understand this blessing. How can I receive God's great comfort if I'm not hurting? How can I draw near to Him without poorness of spirit and mourning?*
>
> *And even those who do not directly have broken circumstances—one glimpse to this broken world should make us mourn, make us poor in spirit. Hurting for healing in Jesus. And shouldn't we want that?*
>
> *Out of overflow of God's comfort and love in my heart, I was able to write those words just a couple weeks after Clive passed. He is such a great Comforter. In the midst of such hurt and*

IT IS QUITE USELESS
KNOCKING AT THE DOOR
OF HEAVEN FOR EARTHLY
COMFORT: IT'S NOT THE
SORT OF COMFORT THEY
SUPPLY THERE.

–C. S. LEWIS

brokenness, there is such an intimacy with Him. From that
intimacy overflows blessing.

I remember wondering how people could enter into that intimacy in other moments of life. How do we do that in the perfect, beautiful, pain-free moments? By recognizing the brokenness around us in the world. Our hurting country, our hurting friends. By entering into that with our brothers and sisters. By seeing the beautiful joy and blessing in that broken dependence. It's not all sack-cloth and ashes, although there is a time for that. In fact, it is such comfort and love and living hope. It is truly life, not the fluff.

We have so many unanswered questions, and we're confused as to why we are traveling what feels like a familiar road again. But, I remind myself, it is a new road with the same Guide. We trust Him.

So many of us never have an answer for our suffering. Even Job, the most notorious sufferer in human history, never knew that his suffering and his continued faith in God—despite enormous hardships—would provide encouragement to people for thousands of years.

In this waiting time, as we pray for Winnie's life and growth, I have an amazing chance to live out (again) what I've learned. I have a chance to hope, trust, lean deeper still into His presence, and receive blessing in the midst. All else fades away.

May I seek total dependence on Him, rather than pursuing stability or the comfort of the world. May I daily surrender everything in pursuit of Him. In that, each day is another one lived in faith and, by God's grace, joy. It's inexpressible and glorious joy.

> *Though you have not seen him, you love him;*
> *and even though you do not see him now,*
> *you believe in him and are filled*
> *with an inexpressible and glorious joy.*
> *- 1 Peter 1:8 (NIV)*

It's a joy that doesn't make sense. Because how could we have joy in the midst of such turmoil? How could we have peace and rest in the wait?

Because, God.

We're not special, and we don't have a remarkable faith. But we do serve and love a remarkable God. A God with wounds, a God who understands, and a God that never leaves us.

As I sit again in this blessing of complete dependence upon Him, I am enjoying the clarity of mind that it offers me. I am allowing time to capture my thoughts and cling to them, that I will not forget this beautiful brokenness. Like Mary, I'm treasuring all these things and pondering them in my heart.

Someday, we'll share these beautiful treasured stories of ours with our children. We'll tell them of God's steadfast love. They will know His goodness.

We are blessed by knowing our need for God and fully experiencing Him. God uses the hurt to draw us to dependence on Him and to remind us of our need to cling to Him at all times. There is beauty in the brokenness.

(Originally shared as a blog post, July 13, 2016.)

REFLECT: Have you ever felt blessed by brokenness and dependence on God? Why or why not?

May your

UNFAILING
LOVE

be my comfort.

- PSALM 119:76 -

When It's Hard to Trust Your Comforter

It's hard to trust a God who seems to have given you false hopes, crushed dreams, and unanswered prayers. It's hard to trust a God who seems to have control over the world but didn't save your loved one. It's okay to wrestle with these thoughts. Pushing them aside won't make them go away.

God's comfort is not a simple comfort. Far from the comfort of self-care and ice cream, it's a deep comfort of the soul. It's a complicated comfort because it's a relationship that must grapple with serious questions. *Is God good? Can I trust Him?*

While there is complex theology to unpack with answers to these questions, I've chosen to press into thought processes and simple reminders that re-orient my mind and heart. I urge you to seek the resources most helpful to your own processing. In my deepest grief, I didn't always have the energy for theology, but I could ponder these thoughts.

Can God comfort me?

> I can allow myself to feel all the emotions of grief and frustration toward God. He can handle my honest feelings.

> I can remind myself of the truth in the scripture. If the Bible feels overwhelming to read right now, I'll simply focus on the Psalms.

Is He even good?

> I have wondered this many, many times. I keep coming back to a simple thought process:

> He made Winnie. She is perfect and good, so He is good.

> He made Clive. He is perfect and good, so He is good.

> He made beautiful things on this earth. Only a good God could create such beauty in the wildflowers and mountains and ocean and animals.

> He is good.

Why do bad things happen?

Death happens. It is a part of this broken world. God allows it, but it isn't what He desires.

Don't discount or discredit the work of the Enemy. He is set on destruction. He has no mercy and knows no boundaries.

If He cares, why did He let my loved one die?

I don't know the why. I may never. I might get glimpses of some good coming from my deep pain, but I won't fully understand why Clive and Winnie had to die. I don't know why your loved one died.

Instead of asking why, I try to focus on "what now?" *How will I allow this deep pain to change me? For better? To become more compassionate, caring, loving? To become less materialistic, less distracted, less filled with the noise and busyness of this world? Or will I allow it to make me bitter, angry, discouraged, and resentful?*

On difficult days, I remember the sweet goodness contained in the souls of my children, and it reminds me of how I want to transform because of their lives. I am better because I knew them; the world is better because they existed. They existed because God created them, and they are His beloved children.

The moments of comfort and peace may come and go. There may still be bitterness, frustration, confusion, and anger. You may continue, as I have, to wrestle through a myriad of emotions on a regular basis. You may wrestle with God and doubt His goodness. You may resist His comfort and feel bitterness. It is normal to feel such a range of emotions, and it is normal to wrestle with God through grief. Although you cannot will yourself to feel His comfort, you can pray for it, try to open up to it, and earnestly pursue Him. It may feel difficult, but as you write or say prayers to Him, pray the words that you hope to be able to say. Speak them, pray them, and maybe someday they will feel more true. Continue lamenting and crying out. He wants to know your heart; He's your Father.

The trauma, pain, resentment, and hurt will not just go away on its own. It can be hidden for a time, but it must be dealt with. In the chapter Faith, we'll discuss more about trusting God. As you work towards this relationship and trust with Him, try to allow Him to comfort you.

As I shared previously, it was difficult to experience God's comfort after Winnie died. I felt utterly alone for months. Slowly I was able to read scripture, listen to worship music, and pray. Often it was forced—just moving through some motions. Other times I approached God with honesty and brokenness. My anger was very real. Sometimes I'd read passages or go to church and walk away dejected. I'd become so worn out by people and discouraged by a message that felt like it had no application for my own life. In time, I processed through these thoughts with trusted friends.

I wish I had a captivating story of remarkable awakening, but healing often happens so slowly I do not even recognize it. Eventually, I woke to see the sun and hear the birds, and I didn't resent life for continuing on. A stranger's smile didn't fill me with bitterness. A hurtful word didn't set me on edge.

Over time my faith began to feel more authentic. Slowly, I felt the comfort of God. My trust returned—still ebbing and flowing like any relationship. Gradually, my eyes opened to see the suffering of those around me, the pain Jesus experienced, and the reality that there is no true and lasting comfort apart from Him. All else fails and fades.

> *You keep track of all my sorrows.*
> *You have collected all my tears in your bottle.*
> *You have recorded each one in your book.*
> *-Psalm 56:8 (NLT)*

Rest in the comfort that He knows and cares for your tears. He counts each one. He is not absent or distant but a loving, good Father who knows us intimately. Allow His comforting balm to soothe your soul and wipe your tears. Even if you cannot experience His comfort yet, pray for it to come. Pray for your heart to be soft and open to God's comfort.

REFLECT: Write out some of your answers to these questions: *Can I be comforted by God? Is He even good? Why do bad things happen? If He cares, why did He let my loved one die?* How can you explore these answers further?

Your ways, God, are holy.
    What god is as great as our God?
You are the God who performs miracles;
    you display your power among the peoples.
With your mighty arm you redeemed your people,
    the descendants of Jacob and Joseph.

The waters saw you, God,
    the waters saw you and writhed;
    the very depths were convulsed.
The clouds poured down water,
    the heavens resounded with thunder;
    your arrows flashed back and forth.
Your thunder was heard in the whirlwind,
    your lightning lit up the world;
    the earth trembled and quaked.
Your path led through the sea,
    your way through the mighty waters,
    though your footprints were not seen.

    —Psalm 77:13-17

Comfort of Community

David grabbed his dad and another pastor after the church service, and we all made our way to the front of the small auditorium.

"These are the friends I told you about. Their son passed away two years ago, and their daughter tragically died last year." Compassionate eyes met mine as he asked his dad to pray over us.

"I imagine it's hard for you to believe right now." We nodded. Strangers surrounded us in the crowded room, chatting about lunch and gathering their children, but for a few holy moments all stood still.

He began praying the Apostles' Creed:

> "We believe in God, the Father almighty,
> creator of heaven and earth.
> We believe in Jesus Christ, His only Son, our Lord."

"I say 'we', because we know that sometimes you can't believe alone. We carry you. Even when you can't believe, we believe for you."

The shame of unbelief, fear of being unseen, and sadness of being misunderstood lifted as these benevolent words met our ears and eased our burdens.

—

We are made for community. God gave us one another to share in joys and pains. We can't get through this alone, and we're not supposed to. Our eyes open to the needs around us, and we throw our arms around those who are hurting—recognizing pain, expressing kind words, and stepping in to help.

Allowing those arms to be thrown around us doesn't come so easily. Accepting help is hard. As we do this, our hearts are open to admit our own inability to take care of everything. Friends and family step in with words, practical help, and sometimes financial support. Don't deprive others of the opportunity to help through your grief journey.

There is unity in suffering. It draws us together because it burns away all the trivial things in life. Grief pulls us towards people who are living their lives with bared hearts. The vulnerability is captivating because it is *real*.

If you feel alone in this time, that's understandable. I had many moments of feeling painfully alone and hurt by the community that I'd felt so loved by just days earlier. Press on toward relationship rather than pulling back. If you haven't had wonderful, supportive friends in the past, this is a time to seek those friendships.

Many relationships will change, but try to find a few people to cling to during your time of grief. These might be new friends from a grief group, Bible study, or workout class. Allow some people into your inner pain and share your burden with them.

You may need to seek some friends who can give you the gift of just being present. Request that they sit and listen to you without giving thoughts or advice, unless you directly ask for it. Just as we can allow God to comfort us, we can allow His people to comfort us.

Praise be to the God and Father of our Lord Jesus Christ, the Father of compassion and the God of all comfort, who comforts us in all our troubles, so that we can comfort those in any trouble with the comfort we ourselves receive from God.
-2 Corinthians 1:3-4 (NIV)

Our family, friends, and church family have held our hands through many things. Some of them have been through great loss. Others haven't, but they've entered our grief in a beautiful, helpful, and healing way. A few of my closest friendships have grown out of seasons of deep pain, as I learned to depend on other people and allow my heart to be vulnerable and open.

A friend leaned in to me and said, "It's like you have access to a secret, terrible club—one you didn't even know existed." She was right. I have a new group, full of people who have also lost little ones. There are so many communities I didn't know existed a couple years ago—many of them online. Although I wish none of them were navigating this path, I've met such loving, beautiful hearts that I would never know if Clive and Winnie had not lived and died. While it may sound strange to desire to surround yourself with hurting people, it is a group that meets me with great understanding and empathy. The world is full of suffering, and God didn't single you out to be the only one to receive it.

I found unexpected comfort as I read the stories of suffering and trials of generations of people who lived before me: Horatio Spafford, Jim and Elisabeth Elliot, Corrie ten Boom, Dietrich Bonhoeffer, and Elisabeth Prentiss. Their timeless words reminded me I am not alone.

I read books by current-day sufferers, too: Joni Eareckson Tada, Vaneetha Rendall Risner, and Nancy Guthrie. Their words, stories, and faith were a great comfort to me.

May you find comfort in the community of Christ and the fellowship of suffering. May you see how entering into the pain of others does not add to your own sorrow but somehow alleviates some of your burden.

REFLECT: Name three people you can openly talk to about your loss. If you don't have these friendships, where can you go to find them?

Job's Miserable Comforters and God's Ultimate Comfort

The Bible introduces us to Job—the epitome of undeserved suffering—and chronicles his loss of home, crops, children, livestock, and health. As I read *The Message* version of Job, equipped with the knowledge of how to understand the role of his friends and the errors in their counsel, I uncovered deep wisdom.[2]

Job is described as honest, devoted, wealthy, and influential. In the wake of his compounded losses, his initial reaction is worship, followed by lament and questioning. His friends begin as wonderful comforters. After traveling a long distance, they cried out, lamented, ripped their clothing, and even dumped dirt on their heads to signify their deep grief. In a gesture of great friendship and love, they sat in silence with their friend for seven days and nights. But then they opened their mouths.

They asked if Job did anything to cause this immense misfortune. Was it unrepentant sin? They pressed into this again and again, preaching the prosperity gospel to a man who has nothing left. Job is accused of having "loose talk" with his laments, then he's blamed for acting too emotional. His friends are uncomfortable with his suffering and pain, so they look for ways to excuse it, reason it away, or fix it. Not all of their advice is wrong—some contains truth. But much of it is misguided and misdirected.

Job cries out:

> *"The worst of my fears has come true,*
> *what I've dreaded most has happened.*
> *My repose is shattered, my peace destroyed.*
> *No rest for me, ever—death has invaded life."*
> *-Job 3:25-26 (MSG)*

Job's friends want him to rise above this grief, and Job says:

> *"Do you think I can pull myself up by my bootstraps?*
> *Why, I don't even have any boots!"*
> *-Job 6:13 (MSG)*

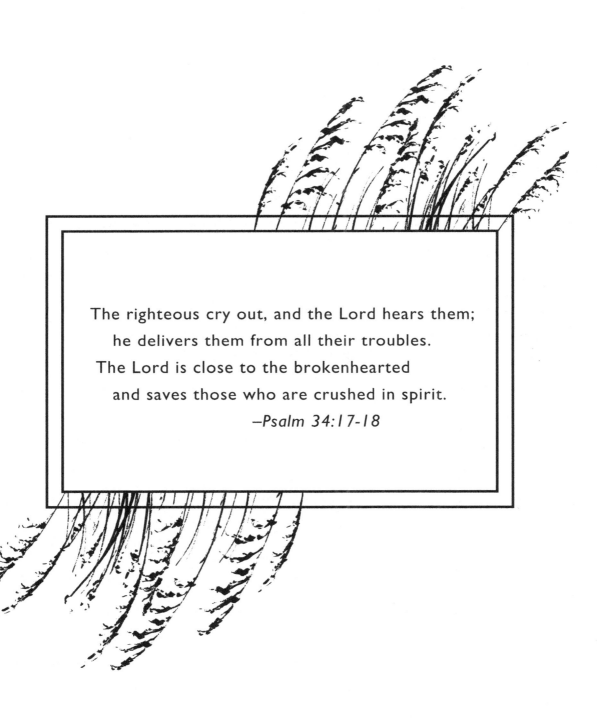

The righteous cry out, and the Lord hears them;
he delivers them from all their troubles.
The Lord is close to the brokenhearted
and saves those who are crushed in spirit.

—Psalm 34:17-18

His friends respond:

"It's plain that your children sinned against him—
Otherwise, why would God have punished them?"
-Job 8:4 (MSG)

Job laments about God:

"As it is, he knocks me about from pillar to post,
beating me up, black-and-blue, for no good reason.
He won't even let me catch my breath,
piles bitterness upon bitterness."
-Job 9:17-18 (MSG)

He is met with:

"What a flood of words! Shouldn't we put a stop to it?
Should this kind of loose talk be permitted?"
-Job 11:2 (MSG)

Job cries out to God:

"Why do you stay hidden and silent?
Why treat me like I'm your enemy?"
-Job 13:24 (MSG)

His friends accuse:

"Why do you let your emotions take over,
lashing out and spitting fire?
-Job 15:11 (MSG)

His friends justify:

"[God] makes us pay for exactly what we've done—no more, no less."
-Job 34:13 (MSG)

Job's words make me groan in sympathy and exclaim "Yes!" There are times I cannot even pull myself up because there's nothing to grab onto. I've had long spells when God feels hidden, leaving me wondering if the pain will ever relent. I fear my laments will be met with comments that shame, condemn, and accuse.

Many people will say and do the wrong things. You may have friends who have spoken to you in harsh, condemning ways. In the chapter Grace, we'll talk about how to handle it. In the meantime, there is truth to glean in the story of Job.

Ultimately, Job's friends could not give him the comfort he desired. You can't solely depend on a person to be your comfort—they will fail you. Your true consolation comes from God.

At the end of the book, God finally speaks to Job from the eye of a violent storm. He draws attention to His glory, calling out Job's ignorance to the Big Story of the world. He even reprimands Job's friends for their lack of help in their friend's suffering.

God says:

"Where were you when I created the earth?"
-Job 38:5 (MSG)

Have you ever ordered Morning, "Get up!"
told Dawn to "Get to work!"
-Job 38:12 (MSG)

"Can you get the attention of the clouds,
and commission a shower of rain?"
-Job 38:34 (MSG)

Job answers:

"I've talked too much, way too much.
I'm ready to shut up and listen."
-Job 40:5 (MSG)

"I've babbled on about things far beyond me,
made small talk about wonders way over my head."
-Job 42:3 (MSG)

"I admit I once lived by rumors of you;
Now I have it all firsthand—from my own eyes and ears!"
-Job 42:5 (MSG)

Ultimately Job's comfort from God was in recognizing his own smallness. It pales in comparison to God's Glory. Sometimes it's good to feel small.

In the midst of Job's extreme pain, God demonstrates that nothing can happen to us that hasn't already happened. Nothing is out of His territory. He has seen the greatest joys and deepest sorrows that mankind has experienced.

God demonstrates His power and strength. The distant galaxies and the smallest cells are under His rule. He is the ultimate authority.

God reminds us of His responsibility as ruler. Would we want the duty of choosing who lives and dies? Would we want the weight of the whole world—and pain of the whole world—to rest on our shoulders?

Job rejects the quick fixes and platitudes from his friends and experiences comfort by encountering his own smallness next to the glory of God. The Maker of the universe, the Creator of mountains and forests, and the Builder of the earth's foundations intimately cares for Job. This is love.

The Lord possesses knowledge beyond our grasp, that which our mind cannot comprehend. Yet He lovingly comforts as He communicates with us through His word. He is the one steadfast friend in our life, the listening ear that does not turn away, and the Father that does not demand justice but demonstrates mercy to His children.

REFLECT: How have you experienced wonderful and miserable comforters in your life? How have you experienced the comfort of God?

Encountering God in His Creation

I watched the sun rise over concrete buildings and the rooftop garden outside our hospital window. The long night was over, and Clive survived. The previous day sent us into a tailspin of an emergency heart surgery and an unknown prognosis. We watched him bleed all night, unable to hold and comfort our one-month-old.

Our moms stayed in the waiting room all night, as we were unwilling to expose them to the horrific sight before us. We stood: helpless, hopeless, and numb as the night dragged on with uncertainty. His team worked around the clock to stabilize his tiny body; life-support machines hummed, and monitors beeped.

But as the sun rose, and the morning met the room, there was a measure of steadfastness in the chaotic world around me. It was a reminder of God's comforting presence. I smiled weakly. Clive's previous room had no exterior window, and at five weeks old he experienced his first sunrise—still with us.

> *Weeping may remain for a night,*
> *but rejoicing comes in the morning.*
> *-Psalm 30:5 (NIV)*

> *The steadfast love of the LORD never ceases;*
> *his mercies never come to an end;*
> *they are new every morning;*
> *great is your faithfulness.*
> *-Lamentations 3:22-23 (ESV)*

Even now the sun continues to rise each day. Sometimes it's hidden by clouds or impossible to see. Sometimes the nights are so dark it's hard to imagine a time of light. But it's steadfastly there.

There are other reminders of God's faithfulness, steadfastness, and comfort. Consider the trees that grow to shade. Remember the rain that comes to replenish. Think of the fruit that grows to nourish. The seasons, the growth and rebirth, the intricate web of nature all entwined together by a Creator God. He is the God who commands the storms and simultaneously catches our tears in a bottle (Psalm 56:8, ESV). Even in our smallness and His largeness, we are fully loved.

As you drive today, look up. As you walk, look around. Listen to the tick of a watch. Although man-made, it provides a steady reminder of the Time Maker and Keeper. See the comfort of God's creation in the patterns and beauty that surround you.

REFLECT: How do you experience God's comfort through His nature and creation?

Turn Your Eyes Upon Jesus

Helen Howarth Lemmel

O soul, are you wea-ry and trou — bled? No light in the dark-ness you see?
Through death in - to life ev - er - last — ing He passed, and we fol - low Him there;
His word shall not fail you-He prom — esed; be - lieve Him, and all will be well;

There's light for a look at the Sav - ior, and life more a - bun - dant and
o - ver us sin no more hath do-min - ion - for more than con-querors we
then go to a world that is dy - ing, His per-fect sal - va - tion to

free!
are!
tell! Turn your eyes up-on Je - sus, look full in His won-der-ful

face, and the things of earth will grow strange - ly

dim in the light of His glo - ry and grace.

Creative Response:

Art Journal Activity: Create a Focus Verse. Pick a comforting verse to focus on for this project. Use a variety of papers, doodles, collage, or paint to create a background for your verse on canvas, cardstock, or in an art journal. You can type your verse or write it out. Using different fonts can help your mind focus on certain words of truth. As you work, pray that the words would become true to you and that God's comfort would be evident to you.

Art Journal Activity: Paint, draw, or use mixed media to create an image of the word *comfort* and what it means to you right now. Is there internal conflict when you consider this word? Do you feel disappointed? Do you feel cared for?

Find a comfort item to remind you of your loved one. It could be a clothing item, blanket, photo, or toy. This can be something you can hold when your heart is feeling broken and when your arms feel achingly empty. There were many nights I fell asleep weeping and clinging to a special blanket that provided some comfort.

Set aside time. As you feel sadness or anger, set aside time to allow these emotions to wash over you and release. Even by opening this book, you are showing that you want to believe and heal. It takes tremendous courage to embrace healing, and you are doing that hard work. It is important to make sure you are not bottling up all your feelings, as they can lead to more stress, anger, aggression, or unhealthy habits. You may need to just sit, cry, or write. You may want to hold a comfort item to remind you of your loved one and God's love for you.

Read Job. *The Message* version by Eugene Peterson is wonderfully paraphrased and understandable. As you read (or listen on the free Bible App), consider Job's honesty, his friends' lack of comfort, and God's glory. Nancy Guthrie's book *Holding onto Hope* takes you through Job and has an excellent Bible study of Job included.

Find and create your next Ebenezer Stone. As I mentioned in the first chapter, building a collection of Ebenezer Stones can provide a physical reminder to you of God's help and deliverance. Look for your next stone today, and label it with a paint marker. You can use a simple word, such as "comfort," a phrase, or anything meaningful at this point in your process. Put it in a spot that will

serve to remind you of God's presence and help.

Find Comfort. Comforting food may be something you long for right now. Fix some favorite recipes for your family. Ask a relative to bring a homemade meal, or ask a friend to pick up your favorite meal from a restaurant. **Comforting moments** could be found by watching favorite old movies, taking time for an old hobby, or spending time outside. **Physical comfort** might be some of the only ways we can feel emotional comfort. After Winnie died, I took plenty of baths to provide physical comfort and calm my mind. A noise machine at bedtime helped quiet my thoughts and aid my sleep. I took long walks to tire my body and prepare it for rest.

Give permission for others to talk about your loved one. Many people are unsure of how to speak with people who have experienced loss. They may fear that bringing up the name or memories of someone who has passed will stir up pain. In reality, however, our hearts are always feeling that pain, and our minds are constantly thinking of them. You may need to express your desires to people if you want them to talk about your loved one. This may look different for everyone. For me, it meant sharing a blog post about still being a mother, still being Clive and Winnie's mother, and letting friends and family know that I loved talking about them and hearing others talking about them.

Seek God in Nature. In my life, God has persistently met me in nature. Feeling the sun on my face feels like the very light of God shining upon me. My soul needs these experiences to draw me back to God. Each of us has ways that God resets and reconnects with us, and it is important to find these ways and make space for them in our lives. Grab your camera and capture some of the beautiful ways God has made the earth. If He is master of the clouds, sun, mountains, and seas, who are we to comprehend His ways? He creates delicate ferns, speckled robin's eggs, and smooth river stones. If He cares for these details, be assured that He cares for you (even when you doubt that, as I have). Allow yourself to sit or stand outside and try to listen to God.

Identify trusted friends you can talk to about your loss. These should be people who will listen to your heart, not try to problem-solve your grief for you. Seek out friends that will listen without offering trite words, thoughts, or advice— and communicate this desire with them. You may already have these friends, or make new connections at a local grief group. Try to schedule a regular time to see people so that you do not have to make the effort to initiate contact with them each time. It is normal for social interactions to be very taxing, so having regular, scheduled times will help it feel less overwhelming. Some days, you may need to cancel. Other days, you might choose to push through and end up being grateful for the time with others.

Identify a local Christian counselor. You may need to ask friends, your pastor, or others you know to help you find a trusted one. It is not a sign of weakness to have a counselor. Even if you do not go immediately or regularly, it is important to have someone available when needs arise.

Please remember: Of course, there are times when the darkness seems to have overcome us, we are having harmful thoughts, or we need help. Medication is a useful tool for that, and you may need to talk to your doctor about it. If you do use medication, I encourage you to continue to seek help from a counselor to continue to work through your grief.

Five Minute Activity: Collecting images of comfort. Use your phone or tablet to start collecting comforting images, quotes, or photos. You could use Pinterest to organize them or simply screenshot them. Take time to look back on these when you need some comforting encouragement.

CHAPTER FOUR

Love

IDENTITY AS A BELOVED CHILD OF GOD

A Shaken Identity

A glance into the mirror revealed a stranger.

Who is she? I wondered, turning to look at my hollow reflection. Pale green eyes met mine, and fear spread through my body. *Was I still there?* I willed my eyes to search for myself within the frame, but my gaze fixed emptily ahead.

Would these eyes know joy again? Could a smile creep across these lips? A juxtaposition of youth and death filled my face, but the person before me remained unrecognizable.

Listless and wandering, the days tumbled forward without Clive. I'd carried him for months, treasuring kicks and rolls. Our hospital days revolved around a tiny boy's bedside as we held hands and sang over him. All my energy had been poured into him for months, and then he was gone.

Who was I without his presence? Was I still a mother? Yes, but not in a traditional sense—I certainly couldn't join the casual conversations with moms around me as they talked about diapers, sleep schedules, and juggling it all. *What about my other roles: wife, friend, daughter, sister, teacher? Could these be shaken, too?* Those are parts of my identity, but they are external—and not permanent.

What cannot be stolen? The question became more important as my identity collapsed.

Underpinning these questions was a deep-seated fear—a pervasive feeling of emptiness, nothingness, and unworthiness. *Could I ever be the same again? Could I ever know love and joy? Do I have value and significance?*

One day after weeks of seeking and not finding, His words met my heart:

"Fear not, for I have redeemed you;
I have called you by name, you are mine.
When you pass through the waters, I will be with you;
and through the rivers, they shall not overwhelm you;
when you walk through fire you shall not be burned,
and the flame shall not consume you.
For I am the LORD your God, the Holy One of Israel, your Savior.
-Isaiah 43: 1-3 (ESV, emphasis added)

I whispered it aloud, speaking Truth to myself:

You are mine. You are mine. You are mine.

It became a constant refrain in the months after Clive's death. In all the confusing, despairing, lost moments, I am His. I am held. I am loved. Remember that you, too, are so loved by God. Even in your questioning, in your emptiness, in your anger, and in your grief, He is still a God who loves you and calls you His child.

REFLECT: What are some titles with which you identify yourself? How has your loss shaken your identity? What are the unshakable truths and identities you can cling to right now?

A New Name

The book rested on my lap in the splayed fashion that would make a librarian cringe. Well-loved in our home, *Hinds' Feet on High Places* once again occupied my morning porch reading time. I drew comfort from the allegorical story which tells of a young woman named Much-Afraid embarking on a journey riddled with pain and suffering. She stumbles on the path as she climbs the mountainside to obtain her new name from the Shepherd.

As I paused to gaze across our porch, watching the sun filtering and rising through the trees, I noted the similarities between our journeys. Much-Afraid is crushed, especially as her mountain-facing path takes a sharp detour into a desert wasteland.

> "I can't go there," panted Much-Afraid, sick with shock and fear. "He can never mean that—never! He called me up to the High Places, and this is an absolute contradiction of all that he promised."[1]

It doesn't feel like love to her as God refines her and allows suffering in her life. As she looks to her traveling companions, Sorrow and Suffering, she wonders if they are true friends and if God is actually good. The journey to a new name is one of struggle and doubt. It's not a straight path.

—

In the Bible, individuals were given new names as their life story changed. We know of Naomi ("pleasantness") changing her name to Mara ("bitter") after the death of her husband and two sons. We know of Abram ("high father") and Sarai ("my princess") becoming Abraham ("father of multitudes") and Sarah ("mother of nations"). We know of Saul ("question") being called Paul ("small"), Jacob ("supplanter") becoming Israel ("wrestles with God"), and Simon ("God has heard") becoming Peter ("rock").[2]

Sometimes God changes our names to redefine our path and character, and other times we change our names to mark a change in our story. However, circumstances do not determine our identity. We are rooted in our identity as sons and daughters of God, and that cannot be stolen from us.

YOUR REAL, NEW SELF WILL
NOT COME AS LONG AS YOU
ARE LOOKING FOR IT.
IT WILL COME WHEN YOU
ARE LOOKING FOR HIM.

—C. S. LEWIS

I've tried to rename myself: bitter, broken, or unloved. I've defined myself outwardly: mother, teacher, or wife. But these are not me; they are a shell of me.

For he chose us in him before the creation of the world to be holy and blameless in his sight. In love, he predestined us to be adopted to sonship through Jesus Christ, in accordance with his pleasure and will—to the praise of his glorious grace, which he has freely given us in the One he loves.
-Ephesians 1:4-6 (NIV)

As He adopted us as His sons and daughters, He gave us His name. Our identity lies with Him and is traced through His family tree—a long legacy of people God has used despite (or because of) their circumstances, losses, inadequacies, doubts, waywardness, and stubbornness.

I'm no longer defined by my jobs, roles, and activities. I'm no longer defined by my actions or my contributions. My identity is secure in Christ. In Him, I am fully known, fully seen, and fully loved just as I am. I am no longer Rachel the teacher, wife, or mother, but Rachel the daughter of the King. *I am His.*

In full transparency, I must admit arriving at these thoughts was difficult after Clive died—it took tremendous energy and intention. After Winnie died, it has continued to be a struggle to wear my new identity. Full of doubt, I cling to the losses and trauma I have endured, thinking they are my true self, but God gently pulls me back to reframe my identity.

Just like Much-Afraid, I continue on up the mountain with my Shepherd. Even when my eyes and heart wander, my weary feet take trusting steps forward. She finally reaches the High Places—the Kingdom of Love—and welcomes the new name of Grace and Glory as the love of God replaces her need for love from other sources. May our journey continue to lead us on a similar path.

REFLECT: What is your name right now? Are you Mara (bitter), Much-Afraid, or Beloved? Who are you becoming? What name would you give your former self, current self, and future self? Explore those ideas by writing a description of who you are under each name.

And I pray that you, being rooted and
established in love, may have power,
together with all the Lord's holy people,
to grasp how wide and long and high
and deep is the love of Christ, and to
know this love that surpasses knowledge—
that you may be filled to the
measure of all the fullness of God.
—*Ephesians 3:17-19*

He restores
MY SOUL.
He leads me
IN PATHS OF
righteousness.
- PSALM 23:3 -

Secondary Losses

The bustling downtown provided plenty of distractions as we walked with coffees in hand. I almost passed the window without taking notice. The large storefront display was filled with soft pinks and leafy greens, and an elegant white gown stood prominently among the blossoms. Tears burned in my eyes, and my heart swelled with pain. My mind raced to catch up to my body's immediate reaction.

My beautiful girl wouldn't ever get married. *Oh, sweet daughter, how I'd love to see your daddy walk you down the aisle.* Even after her death, new and unexpected grief was arising.

When I lost Clive, and then Winnie, I lost them at every age and stage. I lost the opportunity to see their newborn features morph into chubby baby cheeks and thighs. I lost watching their first steps, listening to giggles, and hearing them saying "mama." I missed the chance to put a Band-Aid on her knee and to wipe his sticky fingers. I lost the first day of school, the wedding shower, and the urgent phone call from across the country. Most days I just push through this. How can I not? But a quiet sadness spreads over so many moments. I struggle as I witness growing bellies, peaceful newborns, toddling girls, and rambunctious little boys.

> "Her absence is like the sky, spread over everything."
> –C. S. Lewis[4]

Acknowledging these losses doesn't mean I am dwelling unnecessarily. It means I am healing. A death isn't something you can will yourself to "get over". As I face the impact that grief has on my life—in its many shapes and forms—I am able to move forward rather than stuff these emotions away.

As you adjust to life after the death of someone you love, you encounter loss after loss. Perhaps you lost your traveling companion, your wedding date, or your cooking buddy. Perhaps you lost their future adventures to college, to Europe, or to preschool. Perhaps you lost your home, your financial security, or your sense of normalcy. Perhaps you lost friends who don't know how to handle grief, the ease of lighthearted conversations, or privacy in your life.

As the days pass, we may find more and more ways our lives and our very identities are impacted by grief. Just as the person you are grieving is worth the grief, these secondary losses are also worth grieving. Acknowledging their impact will be helpful in continuing forward with grief and finding your identity rooted in God's love for you.

I will restore to you the years
that the swarming locust has eaten.
—Joel 2:25 (ESV)

REFLECT: What are some secondary losses amidst the loss of your loved one? Some examples are: loss of the future with that person, loss of friends who have walked away, loss of financial stability, or loss of rest. Take time to list these losses and grieve the compounding nature of your loss.

Love takes
off the
masks that
we fear
we cannot
live without
and know
we cannot
live within.

—*James Baldwin*

Heaps of Rubble

I have an affinity for run-down old houses, always dreaming of them in their former glory and hoping to see them restored. My daily commute brought me past one of these homes. As I'd study its peeling paint, sagging roofline, and useless gutters, I'd wonder what would become of it.

One morning it stood—forlorn as ever—and by the time I returned home it was reduced to a pile of rubble. The debris was hauled away, and the next day, it was a leveled lot of dirt. A once-solid home was erased in less than forty-eight hours.

Our own house was foreclosed upon before we purchased it. It reeked of pets. The toilet was broken in half; the plumbing proved entirely useless. Wallpaper covered almost every wall, stained with smoke and grease. The yard was a pile of gravel and concrete pavers.

We slowly restored the home; rebuilding, ripping out, preserving, painting, sanding, and staining. It might have just been easier to knock it down, but we longed to see the home restored to its glory. We noted the sturdiness of the home's foundation, the beauty in its nearly one-hundred-year-old features. *Could we bring life back to the empty shell?*

It took our blood, sweat, and tears. It took our resources, our patience, and our energy. No part happened automatically, and it often looked worse before it got better.

Now a decade later, we have a beautiful and peaceful home. Gardens bloom around the once-barren lot. Photos hang on crisply painted walls; the restored clawfoot tub sits in a renovated bathroom. It's not perfect—it sits a bit unlevel, the windows are exasperating, and it requires the care and upkeep of any old house—but it's home and a far cry from the demolition-ready space it once was.

They will rebuild the ancient ruins
and restore the places long devastated;
they will renew the ruined cities
that have been devastated for generations
- Isaiah 61:4 (NIV)

What Wondrous Love Is This

American Spiritual

arranged by Michael Kravchuk

I sat in a heap of rubble after our miscarriage and slowly allowed healing to happen. It took time and effort, as I took part in the rebuilding and restoration. The walls fell again when Clive died. I found myself again sitting in the debris. I rebuilt sections and healed; I saw hope and joy slowly restoring. The walls fell yet again with Winnie's death, leaving me incredibly defeated.

Healing is hard when it's followed with more pain, damage, and destruction. It's a tiresome burden. A thousand stones surround me, and I'm still just taking one small stone at a time.

It takes time, effort, and intentionality to face the grief. In some ways, it's easier just to ignore it by numbing, tuning out, and distracting myself. But inside, the rubble feels like it's crumbling into further decay. It demands to be dealt with.

There is a reward for this hard work of rebuilding, even if I am unable to see the end product. The bits of grief are dealt with slowly, piece by piece. They are named and released; they are placed and identified; they are recognized and relinquished. One stone at a time, with God as my foundation, living loved and secure with my identity in Him, I am rebuilding. I cannot build on another identity and foundation; it would surely crumble.

Edward Mote penned these words in his timeless song: "On Christ the solid rock I stand, all other ground is sinking sand."[7] My very identity is being rebuilt. Christ is the foundation; nothing else will stand secure. It's the only way I can withstand storms, pressure, and attack.

Will I be shaken again? Perhaps. I'm confident I'll be knocked down at least a little. We live in a broken world. I still think the work of grief and restoration is worth it. Without it, I'd be numb and bitter and cold.

Perhaps I'm getting better at the work of restoration. Perhaps my walls are becoming solidified and reinforced, and the placement of my stones is becoming perfected with time. I'd take another skillset over the skill of grief, but this job is mine to do. I cannot sit in the rubble forever.

I will restore the fortunes of my people Israel,
and they shall rebuild the ruined cities and inhabit them;
they shall plant vineyards and drink their wine,
and they shall make gardens and eat their fruit.
-Amos 9:14 (ESV)

REFLECT: What is the rubble and rebuilding looking like in your life right now?

A God Who Restores Me

As I read about the restoration of the city walls in the book of Nehemiah, I am reminded that God cares about restoring things that are broken. Out of love for us, He desires restoration for our lives.

When Nehemiah, a cupbearer to King Artaxerxes, discovered the walls of Jerusalem had been destroyed and only a remnant survived, he entered deep grief.

> *As soon as I heard these words, I sat down and wept and mourned for days,*
> *and I continued fasting and praying before the God of heaven.*
> *-Nehemiah 1:4 (ESV)*

Nehemiah prayed for four months before he asked the king for permission to leave his job, return to Jerusalem, and gather people together to work on the wall. He was granted permission and assistance, then began the work of gathering people to help rebuild. Side by side, they worked and rebuilt. Each group with their own task in front of them worked together for the greater purpose. It was difficult work as their enemies mocked and attacked. While they worked, they often had a tool in one hand and a weapon in the other to protect against those who were set on destroying their progress.

Their stamina weakened, and they had to depend on God to give them strength.

> *In Judah it was said, "The strength of those who bear the burdens is failing.*
> *There is too much rubble. By ourselves we will not be able to rebuild the wall."*
> *-Nehemiah 4:10 (ESV)*

> *And I said to the nobles and to the officials and to the rest of the people, "The work is great*
> *and widely spread, and we are separated on the wall far from one another. In the place*
> *where you hear the sound of the trumpet, rally to us there. Our God will fight for us."*
> *-Nehemiah 4:19-20 (ESV)*

The wall was completed in 52 days, a miraculous pace for such a huge feat. They had no power tools to move the heavy stones. The wall was intended to protect the city, so it was thick and tall--some parts were eight meters wide.[8] Even managing the seventy-year-old rubble would have been a daunting task. They could have easily abandoned the idea of rebuilding Jerusalem's walls, but they chose to persist. They wanted to see their city restored to its former glory. They knew it was worth it and achievable, regardless of the cost.

It took time, risk, and effort to rebuild the wall, and it also took great effort to rebuild their faith. After the walls were restored, the struggling faith of the people was addressed. Ezra the priest read the book of the law to the people who listened attentively for hours. They wept as they heard the law, and then they took action to restore the commands God had given them: acknowledging and praising God; listening to the telling of the history of their people's faithfulness and waywardness; and confessing and admitting dependence on God.

Even after their desire for complete dependence on God, Nehemiah had to help redirect their rebelliousness many times during his leadership. He reoriented them toward God again and again.

God is a restorer. He desires to see our lives restored and our faith reestablished. Stripped down to the foundation, we are in need of His restoring work. He desires to rebuild us with the foundation of our identity in Christ. He protects us from enemies who seek to destroy us. He patiently reorients us towards Himself as we wander. The stones are too big for us to move alone, but with the help of our God and community we can be rebuilt.

REFLECT: How is God rebuilding and restoring you? How does He do the work of rebuilding by using His community?

Creative Response:

Creator God made us to create. A wonderful part of our God-given identity is creativity. Our God is a creative God, one who cares about the intricacies of the world. He's the creator of neurons, chocolate, thunderstorms, and dandelions. He created patterns and colors and words. He is the master poet, master painter, and master potter. And we are made in His image. You can serve, worship, and grieve through your creativity. How is God revealing His artistry to you? How are you able to glorify God with your creativity?

Self Portrait and Identity Reflection. Draw a picture of yourself or take a picture and print it. Glue it on a background paper. Take smaller pieces of paper and write, use letter stamps, or a printer to capture words to describe your own identity as it exists *right now*. There's no right or wrong; just be honest with yourself.

"You Are His" Ornament. Cut out 3 strips of paper: 1 inch x 5 inches, 1 inch x 6 ½ inches, and 1 inch x 8 inches. They can be on colored or patterned paper. Write out Isaiah 43:1-3 on the strips of paper. You can write on fronts and backs. If you have extra room, write out another verse or a prayer. Fold the pieces in half, then turn the edges inward to form a heart shape. Connect all three hearts together to be three hearts inside one another. Staple the ends together to keep the heart-shaped form.

Art Journal: My Name. Create visual art in your art journal exploring the idea of your name, the name God gives you, and the names you wrongly adopt. Explore the idea of exchange that God grants us in Isaiah 61. He promises to give beauty for our ashes, oil of joy instead of mourning, and a garment of praise instead of a spirit of despair. What does this look like for you?

Art Journal: A House Rebuilt. Write and draw about grief as a house. How does it look now? How did it look before? How is it taking form with rubble, tearing down, and rebuilding? What does the restored home look like?

Find and create your next Ebenezer Stone. As mentioned in the first chapter, building a collection of Ebenezer Stones can provide a physical reminder to you of God's help and deliverance. Look for your next stone today, and label it with a paint marker. You can use a simple word, such as "love," or "identity," a phrase,

or anything meaningful at this point in your process. Put it in a spot that will serve to remind you of God's presence and help.

Establish your role or title. Even after Clive died, I knew I was still a mother (with a very different- looking life than most mothers). I wanted to still be considered a mom, and I wore that role and title proudly even after his death. I had to find ways to 'mother' him and pour my mother-love into something. Would you still like to be considered a mother, sister, daughter, friend, or spouse? You don't have to be ashamed to want to wear that title still. What will it look like? How will you honor their life even as yours moves forward? How can you express this to other people in your life?

Five Minute Activity: Identity Statement. Write an identity statement affirming who you are. You may not believe it now, but write it. Sometimes we have to write things down before we are capable of believing them. Put it somewhere you can see often.

CHAPTER FIVE

Faith

GROWING OUR TRUST IN GOD

Incredible Doubts

A painfully small casket, slightly larger than a shoebox, held a five pound baby girl. My faith shattered as Winnie died, and it felt as if it were buried along with her on that warm August day. Honest, hard, bitter feelings overwhelmed me.

Many Christians do not sense the freedom to express their doubts and pains; it feels too raw to share these intimate thoughts, or wrong to admit uncertainties. Perhaps we fear judgment for questioning our faith and only want to share after the answer has been "found" or peace settles in our souls. Yet, I find myself drawn to the stories written "in the midst" before a lesson is fully understood and before it is tidied up with a pretty, resolute bow.

Overwhelming pain accompanied my faith crisis after we lost Winnie. God's presence seemed distant for a long time, leaving me helplessly alone. Can I share with you some honest doubts from my journal in the wake of Winnie's death?

From My Journal: October 20, 2016—Two months after Winnie died

I've emerged from some really dark confusing days. Last week, I spent Thursday in prayer and reading, and then Sunday I was drained, and Monday was so much worse. Every part of my day went wrong, but even more so, I felt so abandoned by God. I was alone for dinner, and decided to make myself food, something I've had difficulty doing. Dinner almost burned, sauce scalded my hand, my meal spilled all over the couch and on a handmade white blanket. In tears, I could hardly find the strength to clean up. But even more than that, I felt that God let me be further hurt by the Enemy. Lies about how I couldn't be used, how I deserved this, how I needed to learn something. Such complete darkness. Crushed, persecuted, struck down. But not destroyed? It felt like I was destroyed. I sought refuge, but felt I was left in the storm.

My eyes were empty and hollow. When he came home, Sam kept saying he loved me, but I didn't even feel capacity to love him. I felt empty, hopeless, despairing.

Why, even after such purposeful seeking Him, does He allow the Enemy to have a place? I can get through my losses but I cannot get through the abandonment and attacks and darkness. Oh, how different I wish this was.

From My Journal: October 27, 2016—Two months after Winnie died

I felt so encouraged recently, but now it feels like a distant memory. As I lay in bed alone last night, I felt the immense loneliness. Sam fell asleep on the couch, too tired to talk. I took sleeping medicine and tried to sleep, but my soul felt so anguished and alone. Even in my crying out and prayers, I didn't feel God's comfort. Even in my prayers for the darkness and Enemy to leave, I felt no relief. I find that so confusing. Where were you, God? I prayed my heart would stop so that I could go be with Clive and Winnie. How, how, how can I expect to move forward, heal, adopt, parent when I feel so completely screwed up in my head?

From My Journal: November 28, 2016—Three months after Winnie died

The darkness has been really, really evident. I'm struggling to understand how God's presence can feel so absent. Aren't we promised His presence despite being promised nothing else? But what can be said when He is not there? Or at the very least He doesn't seem to be there.

I know I have support, but I do still feel so alone. People are busy. It's hard to reach out and ask for help, or just company. I've been feeling very dark and despairing lately. The compounding grief can only be described as terrifyingly confusing. I'm scared. It's so scary in my head. I'm scared to share how complex, how dark, and how confusing it is. I'm scared that I'm going crazy. I'm tired of being so needy. I'm tired of being so isolated and different from everyone else.

From My Journal: December 5, 2016—Three months after Winnie died

God, where are you? Why, when I call, do you not answer?

As we visited the Buddhist temple in Thailand yesterday, I was struck by the thought of how the former absurdity of bowing before man-formed idols now seemed nearly on par with the absurdity of me returning again and again to a God that hurts me in the deepest way.

But He knows. But He knows. He knows the pain of losing a son. My mind tries to remind me. Sometimes it just doesn't feel that way. It's hard when you feel so absolutely open-handed and it's taken. God chooses to take more. He asks so much of us.

From My Journal: December 23, 2016—Four months after Winnie died

God, it's hard to come to you again and again and again. I come in confusion, in anger, in indignation. I come numb, broken, tired. Why can you not pour out your presence and spirit readily? What must I do? Please, give me a sense of your presence. Help me feel less alone.

Those are difficult for me to re-read as I remember the darkness so clearly. Between those painful entries are flashes of clarity and hope, containing pages filled with verses and prayers of all kinds. I find it helpful to share the dark moments with you because I know many people do not want to express those honest doubts for fear of losing their faith altogether. For me, it was all part of wrestling with my beliefs and surrendering my trust (again and again) to Him.

If you think you're abandoned, take heart. He has not left you. You may feel unloved and forgotten. Like me, you may feel terrifyingly confused. Remember, you're not alone, even when it seems as if you are.

"I have told you these things, so that in me you may have peace. In this world you will have trouble. But take heart! I have overcome the world."
-John 16:33 (NIV)

REFLECT: Write out your honest thoughts and incredible doubts in your darkest moments. You are giving words to these emotions, but it doesn't mean you are turning over power. Rather, by speaking out what is hidden, you uncover darkness, illuminate, and redeem.

I KNOW NOW, LORD, WHY YOU UTTER NO ANSWER.

YOU ARE YOURSELF THE ANSWER.

BEFORE YOUR FACE QUESTIONS DIE AWAY.

WHAT OTHER ANSWER WOULD SUFFICE?

—C. S. LEWIS

Wrestling and Arguing with God

Job says: "Though he slay me, I will hope in him; yet I will argue my ways to his face." (Job 13:15, ESV). There's a popular song that focuses on the beginning of this verse but does not mention the second half. Job miraculously hoped in God (even after unspeakable losses), but he still wrestled and argued with God through his pain.

Job oscillates between despair and hope. I find myself in a similar place on a day-to-day basis. Do I want to be stuck in darkness? Absolutely not. Yet, I choose to allow myself to process these thoughts to have a more secure footing. I reject the desire to brush past my experiences because faith is refined through honest wrestling.

> *I shout for help, God, and get nothing, no answer!*
> *I stand to face you in protest, and you give me a blank stare!*
> *-Job 30:20 (MSG)*

> *What did I do to deserve this?*
> *Did I ever hit anyone who was calling for help?*
> *Haven't I wept for those who live a hard life,*
> *been heartsick over the lot of the poor?*
> *But where did it get me?*
> *I expected good but evil showed up.*
> *I looked for light but darkness fell.*
> *-Job 30:24-26 (MSG)*

God seems distant; darkness surrounds rather than light. *Is the Enemy having his way with me? Am I forgotten and abandoned?* It's painful to witness the world around me, full of hope and growth, as others experience that which I desire most in life. I acknowledge this hurt, bringing it before the One who understands the deepest of agony.

I come with questions, crying out in tearful fits like a tantruming child. He's my dad; He can handle my anger, my frustration, my despair, and my pain. He lovingly guides me when I need conviction, but mostly, He just gives permission to let Him know how I feel. Even as I wrestle with God, I do not desire to abandon Him. A relationship cannot be rebuilt without a willingness to work at it.

Go ahead and be angry. You do well to be angry—but don't use your anger as fuel for revenge. And don't stay angry. Don't go to bed angry. Don't give the Devil that kind of foothold in your life.
-Ephesians 4:26-29 (MSG)

"I believe, help my unbelief."
-Mark 9:24 (ESV)

I wrestle, question, and lament—disoriented—and allow myself to be re-oriented. I cannot let my feelings rule over me, but I also cannot discredit them. So I do the only things I know to do: I process, grieve, create, write, ponder, heal, and ask. I lean into my emotions and listen to what they reveal—simultaneously leaning into Truth and listening to what He reveals. Sometimes God speaks to me through His word, though nature, through music, through other people, or through the Holy Spirit's guidance. I strive to be soft-hearted, to allow my guarded nature to melt and make way for face-to-face communion with God.

Still, I know that God lives—the One who gives me back my life—
and eventually he'll take his stand on earth... Oh, how I long for that day!
-Job 19:25, 27 (MSG)

Like Job, we may never know the reason for our suffering. We can choose to love and trust God despite circumstances beyond our understanding. In the midst of this, we can be drawn closer to the true and constant source of joy.

REFLECT: Do you feel freedom to wrestle in your faith with God? How can you create space for this? How can you allow the Truth to redirect you when you are disoriented?

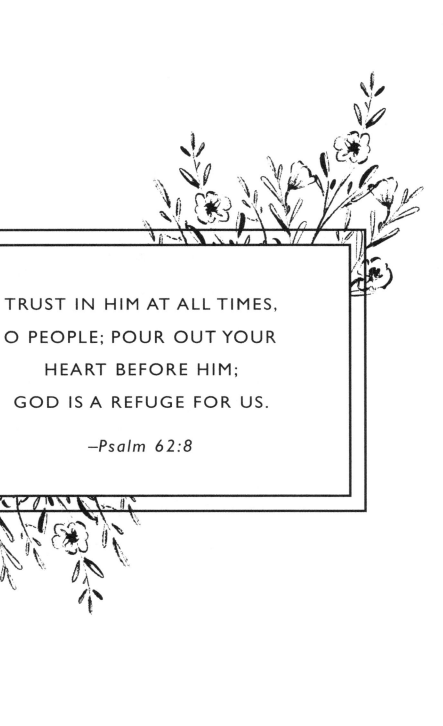

TRUST IN HIM AT ALL TIMES,
O PEOPLE; POUR OUT YOUR
HEART BEFORE HIM;
GOD IS A REFUGE FOR US.

—*Psalm 62:8*

Walking With God

Grief has forced me to reconcile my ideas about faith. I love God but couldn't do much *for* Him in my broken state. Trauma left me sidelined, which contributed to a sense of purposeless existence. Not only had I lost my children, I had also lost many other things—among these, my ability to serve God in the ways I knew how. I was unable to make meals for people, teach Sunday School, lead a small group, or even pray. I was hardly completing the most basic of human functions—eating and sleeping. *How could I serve God when in all practical ways I was useless? Do I lose my value when I cannot give Him anything?*

My mind swings to the other extreme, wondering why God isn't serving my needs. *Why can't He care for me in the ways I see Him care for others? Why doesn't He answer my prayers?* I will be chronically disappointed if I consider all the things that God could do for me and does not do. It isn't fair to consider Him a genie or magician. He doesn't just perform acts of kindness and blessing, but in His sovereignty He is above all things.

He is with me, even if it doesn't feel as if He is doing things for me. He is with me, even if I don't agree with His plan. He is with me, even if I can't serve Him in the many ways I am used to serving Him. *Do I walk away from God when He's not doing what I want? When He's not working within my understanding of His bigger plan? When I'm not getting something from Him?*

Rather than thinking about what God can do *for me* or what I can do *for Him*, I have to remember that we are journeying and walking together. I am with Him, and He is with me.[2] Dropping our expectations of one another, we simply remain in each other's presence. He listens as I cry; I listen as He talks.

"The LORD your God is in your midst,
a mighty one who will save;
he will rejoice over you with gladness;
he will quiet you by his love;
he will exult over you with loud singing."
-Zephaniah 3:17 (ESV)

Then there's the work of forgiving God. *Is this even okay to talk about? Will I be judged?* Of course, God doesn't need my forgiveness, but I needed to forgive Him anyway. I was hurt and angry (some days I still am), and it felt very personal. *Why, out of the whole world, did He give me this lot in life? Why do I have to suffer in this specific way? Does He hate me? Does He love me?* Just as someone has to air their grievances, I had to do so with God.

It took time, but slowly I could see my circumstances from a distance. I could see that there were others carrying similar burdens in losses—I was not alone in suffering. As I watched God extending love to them, I could recognize small examples of His love to me.

Forgiveness looks a lot like trust. Even though He allowed me to be hurt in the deepest way, I forgave. And even though He allowed me to hurt in the same way again, I had to choose to trust.

I don't understand why. I don't accept it willingly, but I see that this is not what God desired or intended for the world. It's a broken place—caused by direct actions of people, the Enemy, and the sickness and brokenness of our own bodies. It's not a personal attack on me because of my sin, nor a personalized suffering to teach me a specific lesson.

The Lord is compassionate and gracious,
slow to anger, abounding in love.
He will not always accuse,
nor will he harbor his anger forever;
he does not treat us as our sins deserve
or repay us according to our iniquities.
For as high as the heavens are above the earth,
so great is his love for those who fear him;
as far as the east is from the west,
so far has he removed our transgressions from us.
As a father has compassion on his children,
so the Lord has compassion on those who fear him.
-Psalm 103:8-13 (NIV)

Reconciling my walk with God was difficult. It continues to require humility,

Be strong
AND TAKE HEART,
all you who
HOPE
in the Lord.
- PSALM 31:24 -

patience, growth, and willingness to see a perspective apart from my own. Yet beautiful and redemptive reconciliation is the goal of relationship. God desires a restored relationship with us, just as He desires a healing in our relationships with others.

REFLECT: How have you had to forgive and surrender to God? List some ways you've felt hurt or betrayed by God. Write down some truths you know of God.

Silence, Solitude, and Listening to the Lord

I crave noise and distraction, even from devotional books, worship music, and podcasts. While helpful, they are no replacement for trying to hear the voice of God speaking to me. I have access to the source of Truth, so why fill my mind solely with the messages from other people?

One practice I've implemented during my grief journey has been listening to God by entering times of silence and solitude. While quiet moments don't always feel feasible in our lives, we can find them in the margins. It might mean a few minutes during nap time, or utilizing early morning and late night hours—instead of reaching for the remote or social media. It might mean surrendering productivity for a few moments of Presence.

Here are some suggestions as you enter into this time:

Sit comfortably. Remove temptations, such as your phone. Close your eyes to limit distraction. Have a journal ready to write. Have a separate paper on hand to jot down random thoughts, distractions, and to-dos as they undoubtedly arise. As you write them down, release them for later.

Focus and redirect your thoughts. Read passages such as Psalm 23 or 46, or Ted Loder's poem "Gather Me to Be with You."

Take a deep breath in and out.

Lord, I breathe in your truth. I breathe out my worries.

Lord, I breathe in your goodness. I breathe out my burdens.

Lord, I breathe in your presence. I breathe out my distractions.

Bring something before the Lord: a worry, a concern, a thought. Lay it down at His feet.

Say a prayer of listening and presence to Him. "Here I am, willing to listen."

Listen. Instead of praying and talking to Him, try to allow Him to speak something to you. Sometimes this might be in images (as it often is for me), or in words. If something comes to mind, ask God what He is telling you or revealing to you through this. Sometimes it doesn't happen, and it's just a time of quiet, stillness, and refreshment; don't consider this a failure. Try to set a timer for ten minutes, so you can really enter into the time of listening. When your mind wanders, refocus it on listening to God, repeating your willingness to listen to Him.

Try to do this regularly, as it will become easier to listen to God and discern His voice.

Take time to reflect on what you have learned or heard. Journal about it and take some time to reflect and process what God is teaching you as you listen to Him.[4]

> *For God alone, O my soul, wait in silence,*
> *for my hope is from him.*
> *He only is my rock and my salvation,*
> *my fortress; I shall not be shaken.*
> *On God rests my salvation and my glory;*
> *my mighty rock, my refuge is God.*
> *Trust in him at all times, O people;*
> *pour out your heart before him;*
> *God is a refuge for us.*
> *-Psalm 62:5-8 (ESV)*

REFLECT: What are some practical ways you can cultivate silence, solitude, and listening to God? Are you fearful to do this? Give your fears to God and ask Him for direction in how to enter into stillness and communion with Him.

Faith is believing
what we do not see,
and the reward for
this kind of faith
is to see what
we believe.

—*St. Augustine*

Legacy of Faith

Do you find comfort in stories of struggle and perseverance? Joseph's story in the Bible is one of long-suffering and faith. At age seventeen, he is undeservingly sold into slavery by his jealous brothers. God was with him and granted him the responsibility of managing Potiphar's household. After working steadily and honestly for Potiphar, Joseph is falsely accused of assaulting Potiphar's wife and imprisoned.

He serves and works in prison, again rising into leadership with God's blessing. Years pass before he is released to interpret Pharaoh's dream about years of harvest and years of famine to come to the land. He proves to be reliable and is elevated to the position of second in command. Years later he faces his brothers again when they come to beg for food during a famine. While they do not recognize him, he eventually reveals himself to them as their brother.

Fourteen chapters of Genesis are dedicated to his life and story, but it seems they do little justice to the length of Joseph's suffering. He was seventeen when he was thrown into a pit and sold as a slave. He served Potiphar for several years, then spent several more in jail. He was thirty when he was finally released to serve Pharaoh. He was thirty-nine when he saw his family again.

Twenty-two trial-filled years had passed. Joseph's faith is never mentioned as wavering or absent. While I imagine he had some doubts, they remain unrecorded. Instead, we have the story of someone enduring hardship, false accusation, and the loss of his family and identity. God granted him favor, but his suffering was exceedingly difficult.

When Joseph reunites with his brothers, they fear punishment for their actions against him.

But Joseph said to them, "Do not fear, for am I in the place of God? As for you, you meant evil against me, but God meant it for good, to bring it about that many people should be kept alive, as they are today. So do not fear; I will provide for you and your little ones."
Thus he comforted them and spoke kindly to them.
-Genesis 50: 19-21 (ESV)

Through his suffering, Joseph sees the bigger picture of his position allowing

You kept my eyes from closing;
 I was too troubled to speak.
I thought about the former days,
 the years of long ago;
I remembered my songs in the night.
 My heart meditated and my spirit asked:

"Will the Lord reject forever?
 Will he never show his favor again?
Has his unfailing love vanished forever?
 Has his promise failed for all time?
Has God forgotten to be merciful?
 Has he in anger withheld his compassion?"

And then I thought, "To this I will appeal:
 the years of the right hand of the Most High."
 I will remember the deeds of the Lord;
yes, I will remember your miracles of long ago.
 I will meditate on all your works
and consider all your mighty deeds.
   —Psalm 77: 4-12 (NIV)

for food to be set aside so that many people would survive. *You meant it for evil, but God meant it for good.*

While I cannot relate in the same measure-for-measure way of knowing God's intention, this idea reveals the way He works in the midst of evil (caused by people, brokenness of the world, and the Enemy himself). God was with Joseph through the suffering and eventually rescued him, restoring his life. Joseph's anguishing story was not forgotten. While it was forever a part of his narrative, he didn't allow the suffering to destroy the rest of his story.

Suffering is often undeserved, unexpected, unwarranted, and unexplained. Joseph's story gives me courage to face the trials in my own life as I am reminded of the steadfastness of the fathers of our faith in the midst of suffering. It humbles me to examine Joseph's faith and trust in God—and it convicts me to lean into my own faith. Unlike many people in history, I have access to God's written word, knowledge of Jesus's sacrifice, the presence of the Holy Spirit, and thousands of years' worth of writing, teaching, and preaching to draw upon. In Joseph's trials, he didn't have access to these things but simply depended on God to sustain him.

REFLECT: Do you draw encouragement from stories of people who have endured long-suffering? Whose story encourages you and reminds you of the gift faith can be in the midst of suffering? Consider people from the Bible, history, or your own life.

Telling Faith Stories

When Sam's parents were younger, they needed a new refrigerator. While providing for a growing family, saving money proved difficult. They tucked cash away for months, saving and sacrificing when they could. Just when they had enough to fund their new purchase, close friends of theirs had a loss in their family. With insufficient funds to fly across the country for the funeral, Sam's mom and dad offered their savings to make it possible for them to go.

About a month later, they received a call from a friend who worked at an appliance store. He had a slightly dented fridge that was the exact model they were saving for and he could give it to them for free.

This story is a simple reminder of God's provision. I've grown to love "refrigerator stories" as they combat my cynical and negative nature. Sometimes these stories are much deeper—our family has stories of remarkable physical healing, incredible relational rebuilding, and unexpected provision and grace. We can't criticize God for the times He doesn't "fix it" and simultaneously withhold the praise He deserves for blessing us beyond measure—in surprising and otherwise inexplicable ways.

So, we tell these stories—as God instructs us in Deuteronomy:

Hear, O Israel: The Lord our God, the Lord is one. Love the Lord your God with all your heart and with all your soul and with all your strength. These commandments that I give you today are to be on your hearts. Impress them on your children. Talk about them when you sit at home and when you walk along the road, when you lie down and when you get up. Tie them as symbols on your hands and bind them on your foreheads. Write them on the doorframes of your houses and on your gates.
-Deuteronomy 6:4-9 (NIV)

These stories give me encouragement. They remind me God cares and provides—even though some life experiences have led me to believe otherwise. I love hearing these simple examples of faith, trust, reliance, provision, healing, and miracles.

We need not avoid telling the other stories, though. Sometimes God does not heal, fix, or redeem *in this life*. As we share both types of stories, we get a glimpse of the full picture and see that He is a God so much bigger than we can imagine. Churches shouldn't singularly reserve their platforms for stories that reveal miraculous healing or provision. Sometimes the most magnificent miracle is the steadfast faith enduring even though the cancer is still spreading.

—

After my first miscarriage, six simple words broke me open: "But even if he does not."

Shadrach, Meshach and Abednego replied to him, "King Nebuchadnezzar, we do not need to defend ourselves before you in this matter. If we are thrown into the blazing furnace, the God we serve is able to deliver us from it, and he will deliver us from Your Majesty's hand. But even if he does not, we want you to know, Your Majesty, that we will not serve your gods or worship the image of gold you have set up."
-Daniel 3:16-18 (NIV)

Reading about this kind of faith—and seeing people all around me live out their own "but, if nots"—has made me brave. God has the power to do anything. Stories from history and from today reveal that. But God also doesn't always do it—our own stories and suffering are evidence to that. *How do we reconcile the two? How do we understand?* I don't think we do. We just trust, knowing our humanity limits our understanding. Remember, it's okay to wrestle with these thoughts. Seek the truth of His word, but allow your mind to press deeply into how God is still good in the midst of pain.

We draw courage and strength from others who are suffering and pressing forward with faith and utter dependence. We cling to these stories of hope, and we learn the power of our own testimony.

REFLECT: List some ways God has been faithful to you or your family. When have you seen examples of physical healing, relational healing, provision, guidance, or protection?

Great Is Thy Faithfulness

Thomas Chisholm   William M. Runyan

Great is thy faith - ful - ness, O God my Fa - ther; there is no shad - ow of
Sum - mer and win - ter, and spring - time and har - vest, sun, moon, and stars in their
Par - don for sin and a peace that en - dur - eth, thine own dear pres - ence to

turn - ing with thee. Thou chang - est not; thy com - pas - sions they fail not.
cours - es a - bove join with all na - ture in man - i - fold wit - ness,
cheer and to guide, strength for to - day and bright hope for to - mor - row:

As thou hast been thou for - ev - er wilt be. Great is thy faith - ful - ness!
to thy great faith - ful - ness, mer - cy, and love.
bless - ings all mine, with ten thou - sand be - side!

Great is thy faith - ful - ness! Morn - ing by morn - ing, new mer - cies I see. All I have

need - ed thy hand hath pro - vid - ed. Great is thy faith - ful - ness, Lord un - to me!

Creative Response:

Spend time in prayer and stillness. Allow examples of God's steadfastness throughout your life to shine through. Write down what comes to mind.

Art Journal: Paths of faithfulness in my life. Use an old map as a background or draw your own. Add in parts to the journey to record evidence of faithfulness, either literal or figurative.

Write out evidence of God's faithfulness. Speak these stories aloud to others and ask them to tell you theirs. Tell your own stories of how He has worked miracles and shown love to you. Remember and cling to these stories, even when other miracles have not happened and prayers have not been answered in the way you would have chosen.

Find and create your next Ebenezer Stone. As mentioned in the first chapter, building a collection of Ebenezer Stones can provide a physical reminder to you of God's help and deliverance. Look for your next stone today, and label it with a paint marker. You can use a simple word, such as "faith," a phrase, or anything meaningful at this point in your process. Put it in a special place.

Sew something by hand. Sewing, especially with old fabrics, reminds me of the legacies and stories of perseverance in my own family. Consider creating a pillow, quilt, or simple sewn artwork. As you work through the stitching, ask God to reveal His Truth to you. Take the time to focus on your task, and ignore all the busyness surrounding you. Consider the ways that sewing can create something beautiful from scraps. Every stitch is purposeful in bringing the pieces together and holding them firmly in place.

Create a faith tree. Write examples of God's faithfulness on paper leaves or dried leaves. Tape a paper cutout of a tree to your wall or place a bundle of branches in a vase. Tape or tie the leaves onto the "tree". If you'd prefer, consider creating a sketched tree in your journal. Add more leaves as you are reminded of more evidence of His faithfulness. Read them on the days that you are feeling full of darkness and doubt.

Five Minute Activity: Free-flow drawing. Grab a pen and some plain paper. Draw whatever comes to mind when you consider these questions: Where is God? Where am I? What connects us, separates us, and draws us together?

CHAPTER SIX

Hope

LIVING IN HOPE & AWAITING HEAVEN

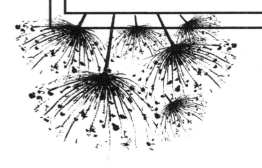

Imagining Heaven

I stepped forward on the trail, eyes focused on my feet treading over rocks. Ferns poked out from crevices, flourishing unexpectedly. The hot late-summer sun was blocked by a canopy of leaves overhead. The forest was alive, abundant, and serene. *Is this what Eden was like? Is heaven like this?*

As I walked on, my mind wandered, as it often does, towards Clive and Winnie. While it's hard to imagine them on streets of gold, picturing them playing among the trees and flowers brings a smile to my face. I envisioned light and warmth. I imagined trails and ferns and beauty surrounding them. Peace was abundant; the presence of God was everywhere. Other children and people were with them, and they were singing together. While I don't know if there's complete validity to these images, they provide comfort and joy to me.

The Bible provides us with many descriptions of heaven:

> a rainbow encircling the throne (Revelation 4:3),
>
> surfaces decorated with precious stones and gems (Revelation 21:19),
>
> a city with gates consisting of large single pearls (Revelation 21:21),
>
> a sea of glass, clear as crystal (Revelation 15:12),
>
> God's face creating light—like the sun shining in all its brilliance (Revelation 21:23),
>
> voices of ten thousand times ten thousand angels singing praise (Revelation 5:11),
>
> a great multitude from every nation, tribe, people and language (Revelation 7:9),
>
> streets made from pure gold (Revelation 21:21),
>
> home to the tree of life and river of the water of life (Revelation 22:1-2).

These images are hard to visualize because they are beyond our own understanding of life and reality. The human language fails to express the mighty wonders we will behold in Paradise someday. I liken it to the monochromatic to technicolor transformation in *The Wizard of Oz*—as Dorothy leaves gray Kansas prairies behind, she enters the unimaginably vibrant, yellow-brick Land of Oz.

We lack the understanding of how different heaven will be from earth, but I imagine our spirits will become so accustomed to it that we will be unable to remember our former, duller dimension of life. We will be filled with and surrounded by perfection.

Meanwhile, as we live and breathe on this planet God created, we are able to bear witness to His glory around us. There are glimpses of heaven here on Earth:

> the soft skin of a newborn,
>
> the breathtaking grandeur of a mountain,
>
> the beautiful diversity of the people of earth,
>
> the magnificent sound of an orchestra,
>
> the stunning colors of a sunset,
>
> the fragrant beauty of a field of wildflowers.

You might even find a glimpse of heaven in an unexpected place. My friend Sarah's son, Angel, had life threatening medical issues his life entire life. When he was nearing the end of a long battle with cancer, his parents spoke to him about heaven. Because he loved playing video games, he asked his mom if there would be video games in heaven. *Valid question for a teenager, right?* His mother's answer has always stuck with me: "I'm not sure if there will be video games in heaven. But that feeling you get when you play video games? You'll have that feeling all the time." Angel smiled contentedly.

Yes. Glimpses of Glory all around us.

On the days I feel broken by life—both my own trials and the greater struggle of humanity in this world—I cling to these bits of Glory among us. I slow and stop. I listen and watch, ever the learner of God and His creation. I think of the beauty that He has created and how much greater still heaven will be. All the beautiful things in the world reflect the beauty of God because He is the maker and beholder of all beauty.

They will enter Zion with singing;
everlasting joy will crown their heads.
Gladness and joy will overtake them,
and sorrow and sighing will flee away.
-Isaiah 35:10 (NIV)

REFLECT: What do we know of heaven? What do you picture when you think of your loved one in heaven?

THERE ARE FAR BETTER
THINGS AHEAD THAN ANY
WE LEAVE BEHIND.

-C. S. LEWIS

Clinging to Hope

There's a human instinct to cling to hope even in the midst of the most heart-breaking situations. Hope can help us withstand great suffering as we look forward to a future without pain. If you were to read through accounts of some of the most severe hardships in human history, many people endured long-suffering with their eyes fixed on the Lord.

Horatio G. Spafford wrote the hymn "It Is Well with My Soul" after losing his fortune in the Chicago Fire, his young son to scarlet fever, and four young daughters in a tragic shipwreck.[2] He penned the words to the famous hymn as his ship passed over the waters of the vessel's wreckage.

The final verse reads:

> *And Lord, haste the day when the faith shall be sight,*
> *The clouds be rolled back as a scroll;*
> *The trump shall resound, and the Lord shall descend,*
> *Even so, it is well with my soul.*

Like many others, Spafford's life did not become easier after experiencing such hardships. He went on to lose a second son to scarlet fever and was eventually rejected by his church leaders for the seeming "divine judgement" that God had cast on his family.[3] Even so, he set his heart on things above and hoped for the restoration to come. *Even so, it is well with my soul.*

—

Throughout our time in the hospital, we hoped and prayed for healing. We sensed the seriousness of our situation as specialists filed in and out of the room—hematologists, cardiologists, pulmonologists, neurologists—yet we clung to hope. We held our son's hand and begged God to spare his life.

In the end, Clive's healing came in a different way: complete and perfect healing in heaven. Although we selfishly desired healing in the physical sense, our hope was not disappointed.

He will wipe away every tear from their eyes,
and death shall be no more,
neither shall there be mourning, nor crying, nor pain anymore,
for the former things have passed away.
-Revelation 21:4 (ESV)

We have a promise of something far greater. We have a promise of a place where there is no death, crying, pain, or mourning. It's impossible for us to imagine this perfect place that lacks so much of what we are familiar with in this broken world. Someday we'll see this full restoration. For now, we wait and cling to the hope of future promises.

REFLECT: How are you clinging to hope? What strikes you about the Spafford family's story?

Awaiting a Heavenly Country

The book of Hebrews provides examples of people of faith awaiting promises: Abel, Enoch, Noah, Abraham, Sarah, Isaac, Jacob, Joseph, Moses, and Rahab.

Now faith is confidence in what we hope for and assurance about what we do not see.
-Hebrews 11:1 (NIV)

All these people were still living by faith when they died. They did not receive the things promised; they only saw them and welcomed them from a distance, admitting that they were foreigners and strangers on earth.
-Hebrews 11:13 (NIV)

Instead, they were longing for a better country—a heavenly one.
-Hebrews 11:16 (NIV)

The chapter is full of stories of people who struggled here in this world yet hoped for heaven. They desired fulfillment of promises, restoration, and land. Although they lived by faith, they did not receive these things during their lifetime. Even still, they kept their eyes ahead to their future home of heaven.

We live by faith, and this means we might not receive things "promised" in this life. This is a hard truth for me, as I remember my babies in heaven and know that life will continue to be different from my expectations. We aren't promised much in this life aside from God's presence. We are misled to believe we are promised health, security, family, financial blessings, a home, and fulfillment of our dreams. These things may happen, but even for the dutiful, tithing, humble, and "upright" family, hardship will come.

One of the Enemy's greatest goals is distracting us from these truths. We begin to believe that worldly blessings are a sign of God's blessing on us. Therefore, we believe that a lack of worldly blessings is God's favor withheld. Our eyes become fixed on the temporal, and we drop our gaze from the heavenly country.

Instead of believing these lies, may our hearts be filled with the promise of His presence, and may our gaze be fixed on our eternal home, no matter what

Life has become a little less sweet,

death a little less bitter,

and heaven a little more real.

—*Puritan Proverb*

HE WILL
wipe away
EVERY TEAR
from their eyes,
AND DEATH
shall be
NO MORE.
- REVELATION 21:4 -

our lives look like today. May our desire for the hope of heaven grow as we wait.

> But those who hope in the Lord
> will renew their strength.
> They will soar on wings like eagles;
> they will run and not grow weary,
> they will walk and not be faint.
> -Isaiah 40:31 (NIV)

REFLECT: When you read Hebrews 11, how do you feel knowing these people lived with hope for something unseen? What are some lies you've believed about promises? How have you been disappointed?

"Hope" is the thing with feathers -
That perches in the soul -
And sings the tune without the words -
And never stops - at all.
—Emily Dickenson

All Things New

Here on earth, everything is bent towards decay. Without care and upkeep, physical items fall into disrepair. The second law of thermodynamics confirms that fact: everything in the universe is moving towards disorder and chaos.

A newly constructed home will need updates and upkeep within the next decade. A new car will need repairs within a few years. A garden will have weeds growing within the season. A freshly washed window can have fingerprints within moments.

Yet God promises all things will be made new: no sickness, no pain, no sin, no darkness, and no falling into disrepair-- only light, love, goodness, glory, worship, and restoration. It's hard to imagine that there will be a time where disease and destruction do not run rampant, but we are promised this.

> *And he who was seated on the throne said,*
> *"Behold, I am making all things new."*
> *Also he said, "Write this down, for these words are trustworthy and true."*
> *-Revelation 21:5 (ESV)*

Jesus began a new work when He came and died. It was the start of restoration, and He provided hope for ultimate restoration. It was the start of redemption, and He provided hope for the ultimate redemption. We are in the in-between, knowing that the new thing has begun, but is not fully finished.

Revelation tells us of a place with no more tears, crying, or pain. It tells us of a new heaven and a new earth. *Behold, He is making all things new.*

REFLECT: What are some things of the world you long to leave as you pass into heaven? What are some things you long for in heaven? Share your hopes and longings with God. Consider sharing with a trusted friend.

Living in Hope

As we wait and long for this heavenly country, our lives do not stop moving here on Earth. After profound loss, there is a desire to exit this world. As C. S. Lewis wrote, "If I find in myself a desire which no experience in this world can satisfy, the most probable explanation is that I was made for another world."[5] There's a beautiful freedom in having confidence in something far greater ahead.

Yet here we are breathing and moving, living another day. Life has shifted course, and, as difficult as it is, we must continue to carry hope into our future. This hope is not just for someday in heaven; it is also for daily sustenance here and now. You cannot endure suffering without hope.

We must live each day with the imperishable hope we receive from our faith. This hope is not circumstantial. This living hope of walking life alongside Jesus brings us joy. If we put our hope in anything else, whether it is family, success, health, career, possessions, or friends, it can be taken from us. However, our hope in Christ's love and sacrifice for us can never be stolen. May we live our lives continually being reminded of this hope and clinging to this truth.

Brothers and sisters, we do not want you to be uninformed about those who sleep in death, so that you do not grieve like the rest of mankind who have no hope. For we believe that Jesus died and rose again, and so we believe that God will bring with Jesus those who have fallen asleep in him.
- 1 Thessalonians 4:13-14 (NIV)

Having a living hope means we don't have to live in darkness and fear. We don't have to dread. We hope for heaven, but we *live in hope* now. We have hope for final restoration, and we have hope for final understanding. We pray for glimpses of both today. Some days, when darkness and fear and dread creep in, we pray and wait *for* hope when we cannot wait *with* hope. Eventually the hope will come more readily.

REFLECT: What does living in hope look like for you? What are some things you hope for in your future here on earth? How will you allow your experiences to change and shape your future here on earth?

Hard to Hope

I returned home from a grief workshop, mug in hand. In beautiful script it read, "There is always hope." I loved and hated it all at once. I wanted to believe but struggled immensely. *But really, is there hope?* It was only a few months after Winnie died, and I began to experience my hardest moments. I doubted everything. I wanted to die. God felt silent. I had almost no hope, and in some moments I had none.

One day, as Sam handed me a morning coffee in that mug, I had an urge to smash it on the floor. His innocent gesture seemed to mock my lack of hope. I became angry and frustrated as I compared myself to people who seemed to possess hope and joy no matter the storms they faced.

> *Hope deferred makes the heart sick, but a longing fulfilled is a tree of life.*
> *-Proverbs 13:12 (NIV)*

Hope has ever-so-slowly resurfaced in my life. It's hard and scary to hope. It feels vulnerable and crushable. Some days I feel hopeful, and other days I feel despairing. Even years later, my soul readily vacillates between the two extremes. I have a strange peace with that.

I push through, much like an athlete completes the hard work of training despite soreness and fatigue. She rests when injury strikes but perseveres whenever possible. Healing is active not passive. I allow myself to see God's miraculous hand in it, but I also have to take responsibility for my own thoughts, actions, and processing. Now, most days, I'm able to smile quietly at my hope-mug as it reminds me of where I've been and where I am.

I strive for honesty as I face my thoughts, and I would never want this book to brush over pain with trite answers. Tiny embers of hope may exist some-where inside of you. I can't create the flames of hope for you, but I can direct you to God, to creativity, to expression and processing, and to resources that have helped me in my journey. Time will not fix it, but time accompanied by some hard grief-work will help make it better.

Healing comes in small, steady steps, not giant leaps. Draw strength from knowing you have survived so much already. Draw strength from God's promises of healing in heaven. Draw strength from the men and women around the world who are persevering through suffering and trauma.

I remain confident of this:
I will see the goodness of the LORD
in the land of the living.
Wait for the LORD;
be strong and take heart
and wait for the LORD.
-Psalm 27:13-14 (NIV)

REFLECT: When has it been hardest to hope? What is your hope deferred? What helps you when you are feeling most hopeless?

It Is Well With My Soul

Horatio G. Spafford

Philip P. Bliss

Creative Response:

Find, create, or buy a remembrance object. While you have hope of reuniting in heaven, it may feel so far away. Sometimes there is comfort in having an item that reminds you of your loved one such as jewelry, a blanket, a picture, or another personal item. It will never be a fair substitution, but it may provide comfort in knowing that as life moves forward you will never forget your loved one. Ornaments are a great way to remember your child and can be a wonderful gift for other friends and relatives who would love a remembrance object, too. Other examples might be: a necklace or locket, a picture, a key chain, a mug, a teddy bear, a symbol, or a scent.

Write a letter to your loved one. Tell them of the hope you have for your future, both here on earth and in heaven. Tell them of the glimpses of heaven you see in your daily life, in nature, in people, in art, or in music.

Choose a song and verse of hope. This can be something that you come back to when you need a reminder of truth to anchor you. Write the lyrics or verse onto a piece of artwork and display it somewhere where you need to be reminded of hope.

Write a letter from your loved one's perspective in heaven. Tell of God's abundant love, of the joy experienced in complete worship, and of the peace of his presence. Imagine the beauty that surrounds your loved one as they are held by our Father.

Art Journal: Create an image of heaven. Consider the words, colors, or images that fill your mind when you picture this beautiful space. Use painting or mixed media to create this in your art journal.

Find and create your next Ebenezer Stone. As mentioned in the first chapter, building a collection of Ebenezer Stones can provide a physical reminder to you of God's help and deliverance. Look for your next stone today and label it with a paint marker. You can use a simple word, such as "hope," a phrase, or anything meaningful at this point in your process. Put it in a spot that will serve to remind you of God's presence and help.

Create a beacon of hope to display in your home. It could be artwork, a verse, a plant, or something beautiful that reminds you of the hope that you have—both

for this life and for the future. When you see it, pray for hope to be present in your day-to-day life.

Five Minute Activity: Looking to the Future. Make a list of three to five upcoming events that you're looking forward to. They might include dinner out, a play, a movie you've wanted to see, seeing a friend, buying a new book, a change of seasons, or a special day at work. Add them to your calendar. While they might not seem like grand events, they may help you look to the future with a little less fear and a little more anticipation.

CHAPTER SEVEN

Grace

FREELY GIVEN & FREELY RECEIVED

Freely Given to Us

The process of freely giving grace to others must begin in our own understanding of receiving grace from God. We, in our sinful, undeserving position, are granted full forgiveness from a God who knows the deepest parts of our soul and still chooses to love us. The same God who proclaims harboring hatred in our hearts is equal to murdering our brother (1 John 3:15) allows forgiveness for all of us who are undeserving. Recognizing how unworthy we are of His grace opens our spirits to give grace to those around us.

When you're hurting, all the grace-talk feels irrelevant to your current pain. *Oh yeah, I need forgiveness? Must I be reminded of my sins and mistakes? There's yet another standard that I fall short of and grace for my constant failings?* No, love, it's not that. It's that God, in His infinite grace, sees you as His child. Gently cupping your face in His hands, He meets you in the sadness. He does not come laden with burdens and expectations. He takes the heavily loaded pack that you shoulder onto His own back and walks hand-in-hand with you through streams and desert-land, through forests and darkness, up precipices and in blooming meadows. He gives you grace not only for your mistakes but also for your brokenness.

> *"Are you tired? Worn out? Burned out on religion?*
> *Come to me. Get away with me and you'll recover your life.*
> *I'll show you how to take a real rest.*
> *Walk with me and work with me—watch how I do it.*
> *Learn the unforced rhythms of grace.*
> *I won't lay anything heavy or ill-fitting on you.*
> *Keep company with me and you'll learn to live freely and lightly."*
> *-Matthew 11:28-30 (MSG)*

REFLECT: How has grace been given to you by God? By others? What is God teaching you about grace? What lies are you having to fight against?

Greater Grace

I sat in the September grass, a blanket spread under me and the blue sky overhead. With a few hours dedicated to silence and solitude with God, I welcomed the opportunity to hear His voice. As my eyes closed, the filtered light cast a red glow through my eyelids.

After my mind chased away distractions and settled into silence, I had a clear image of parched, barren ground. A well was being drilled into the earth, but the water reservoir was difficult to reach. As the drill plunged deeper to meet the water below, the empty tunnel grew dark and ominous. My visualization became burdensome and exhausting as I wondered what would happen next. Finally, the dark tunnel filled with a spring of fresh water swelling from the deep well. Water forcefully rose and burst forth, reviving the cracked ground with moisture.

As I sat quietly and asked God what this meant, the words "greater grace" were impressed upon me. I would need to draw into deep reserves, even deeper wells of grace for my present moments, my profound grief, and my anguish. The grace I'd needed in earlier parts of my life was simpler and easier to reach. This greater grace was hard-sought, yet it would be lavished on me as my needs became increasingly compounded.

We are told His grace is sufficient for us, and His power is perfected in weakness (2 Corinthians 12:9). Not only is it sufficient, but it is also abounding. It dwells deeper and bursts forth. As God supplies this grace-gift, I need to be willing to receive it. It is not merely grace for my own struggles and sins but also grace to cover the brokenness in the world and all the work of the Enemy.

A few months later, deeply hurt by a situation involving my grief and a loved one, I pressed into this greater grace and received encouragement from the reminders God had given me.

From My Journal—After a hurtful situation

I felt in a big funk so far today, depressed and angry, and just kept thinking I DON'T WANT TO HANDLE THIS WITH GRACE. I'm tired of being that person that just prays through these hard situations, who kindly responds to things people hurt me with. But then I began to wonder... what good would anything do if I handled it differently? If I had an outburst, it would only make it worse. If I became confrontational, it would not help. This is a burden I have to carry, however hard, and even after Clive and Winnie's deaths there continue to be hard burdens I will shoulder. God, give me grace—even greater grace.

"Bear with each other and forgive one another
if any of you has a grievance against someone.
Forgive as the Lord forgave you."
-Colossians 3:13 (NIV)

REFLECT: Consider an extremely painful moment. How can you press into greater grace in this?

RELYING ON GOD HAS TO BEGIN

ALL OVER AGAIN EVERY DAY

AS IF NOTHING HAD YET BEEN DONE.

–C. S. LEWIS

Grace to Trust Their Hearts

I stood, following suit with the surrounding people. As lyrics displayed on the screen, voices rose in unison. My mouth grew dry. The heavy heart within me didn't believe these words right now. If I tried to sing them, I might just crumble in front of everyone.

I felt out of place in community, and the vulnerability of attending church magnified that. It was as if a severe burn stretched across all my skin. It hurt to be left alone without balm. But it hurt to be touched and bandaged, too.

C. S. Lewis mentions this in *A Grief Observed*:

> "I see people, as they approach me, trying to make up their minds whether they'll 'say something about it' or not. I hate if they do, and if they don't."[2]

It's the perfect paradox—it hurts to recognized; it hurts to be ignored. I found myself putting people in impossible situations—I'd resent them either way.

While I don't know your story, I understand the many layers of pain and hurt. There may be people who have purposefully wronged you and cut you down. Perhaps family members accidentally did something but are unrepentant. You might have friends who hurt your heart deeply but do not know. Forgiveness seems especially hard in the context of grief because it can't simply be remedied, replaced, and made well. The pain of death cuts deeply even with the hope of heaven. Still, we must forgive those around us. Processing through forgiveness is such a difficult task, and one that needs much wisdom and strength from the Lord.

Let all bitterness and wrath and anger and clamor
and slander be put away from you, along with all malice.
Be kind to one another, tenderhearted,
forgiving one another, as God in Christ forgave you.
-Ephesians 4:31-32 (ESV)

Shortly after Clive died, I shared my heart with a dear friend, allowing her to see the hurt I had experienced in other relationships. Processing and forgiving

Forgiveness is the key that unlocks the door
of resentment and the handcuffs of hatred. It
is a power that breaks the chains of bitterness
and the shackles of selfishness.

—Corrie ten Boom

He heals the
BROKEN-HEARTED,
and binds up
THEIR WOUNDS.
- PSALM 147:3 -

was proving difficult, and I felt helplessly stuck. She told me that sometimes the best thing to do is "trust their hearts." These wise words have often turned my festering resentment into a posture of grace. Of course, this did not come quickly or easily. It did, however, help me remember that the words people say are often well-intended and come from a caring heart.

Sometimes comments need to be addressed humbly, yet directly, to share how our hearts hurt. These opportunities allow our friends or family to recognize the complexities of grief and learn from the experience. Many times, however, I realized that the correct action on my part was to "trust their heart" and lovingly move forward in grace. No one will fully understand how I feel in loss, and coming to that realization helps me view others in love. I've also become aware of the instances I did not say or do the right thing myself, unknowingly hurting someone with my words or actions. As I hope for grace to be given freely to me in these situations, I must also be generous with the grace I give others.

With time and with a bit of mental reframing, I have found restoration in relationships—the burn is still there, but the pain is lessening with balms and bandages. I have recognized the impact of grief and released my tendency to feel personally affronted. It's neither their fault nor mine; it results from the brokenness of the world. It's another loss—the loss of simple relationships, the loss of regular life.

Let us then approach God's throne of grace with confidence,
so that we may receive mercy and find grace to help us in our time of need.
-Hebrews 4:16 (NIV)

REFLECT: When you consider the moments that cause anger to stir in your heart, which people come to mind? Why? Try to uncover the root of that anger without further stirring it up. How can you grow to have gracious assumptions of those around you?

Nuances of Forgiveness

"Mrs. George, he hit me!" she said, her five-year-old face streaked with tears. The young boy hung his head in admission and shuffled over.

"What happened?" I asked.

"She was in my space. I didn't like the way she was doing it, and I wanted her to move." The conversation continued as we quickly worked through a better solution.

"Okay, what do you need to say to her?"

"I'm sorry for hitting you," he muttered.

Without missing a beat, she replied, "It's okay!" and turned to leave. I grabbed her hand and gently pulled her back into the conversation.

"Actually, it's not okay. He shouldn't have done that. You can still forgive him, but let's remember that it's not okay. Ask him not to do it again." I saw a little flicker of understanding in her eyes as she told him it's not okay, but she forgave him anyway.

It isn't entirely different as adults. In anger, we cry out our wrongs. Afterwards, we often either choose not to accept someone's apology or believe we have to accept the apology and the action both as permissible. There's another choice: we can let the experience teach us, and hopefully them, to do better next time.

He heals the brokenhearted and binds up their wounds.
-Psalm 147:3 (NIV)

Sometimes people hurt us—again and again.

> Perhaps it's the deafening silence and seeming lack of compassion as a close family member allows months to go by without expressing sympathy or checking in.

> Maybe it's the friend who gives constant platitudes or spiritual encouragement that feels unkind.

> Or perhaps someone has asked you to stop talking about your loved one.

Maybe it's a loved one who wants you to "feel better" and "be yourself again," complaining of how you've changed.

It could be the friend who is uncomfortable with your grief and has dropped all communication.

Or the coworker who has compared your loss to that of their beloved pet or son leaving for college.

Maybe it's a boss who gripes about your performance the last few months.

Or a close friend who forgets an important anniversary.

No matter your loss, those around you will fail to be perfect. They will hurt and disappoint you. Sometimes you can handle their blunders with gracious assumptions, but sometimes you need to take action. I have a tendency to try to remedy this situation with a simple response: teaching them. They don't do better until they *know better*. While it feels unfair to help others understand grief when I'm in the midst of deep grief myself, the responsibility helps my attitude towards others.

Many people fear hurting you or saying the wrong thing. Some people act selfishly, as if they worry that death is contagious. Others are uncomfortable with emotions and sadness. We don't have to shoulder their emotions, but we can relegate responsibility by teaching them what we know.

Perhaps we tell them we're already thinking of our children all the time, and that bringing them up won't hurt us more. It might help to tell them their words hurt us and why. We can teach them the helpful things they can do instead of the things they shouldn't do. By taking the time to examine ourselves and transfer that knowledge to those around us, we give them the opportunity to learn. Not everyone will be an appreciative learner, but many will.

At times, we have to create distance between ourselves and others. Having healthy boundaries can help our healing journey. Perhaps this will mean limiting social media and making the choice to stop replaying hurtful conversations. While we can't insulate ourselves from everyone who could cause hurt, we can have wisdom in recognizing appropriate boundaries.

REFLECT: What are some ways you can teach others about your grief? What are some boundaries you may need to consider in relationships?

Blessed is the one
    whose transgressions are forgiven,
    whose sins are covered.
Blessed is the one
    whose sin the Lord does not count against them
    and in whose spirit is no deceit.

When I kept silent,
    my bones wasted away
    through my groaning all day long.
For day and night
    your hand was heavy on me;
my strength was sapped
    as in the heat of summer.

Then I acknowledged my sin to you
    and did not cover up my iniquity.
I said, "I will confess
    my transgressions to the Lord."
And you forgave
    the guilt of my sin.

Therefore let all the faithful pray to you
    while you may be found;
surely the rising of the mighty waters
    will not reach them.
You are my hiding place;
    you will protect me from trouble
    and surround me with songs of deliverance.

–Psalm 32:1-7

A Million Moments of Forgiveness

In our premarital counseling, we scored "highly compatible". We were great at working side-by-side—serving together, renovating together, teaching together, eating together, even folding laundry together. Then we miscarried, and started a business, and Clive died, and Winnie died, and we lost our synchrony along the way. We argued about everything. Each decision was agonizing to make; we never agreed. We'd lash out at one another, using the other as a scapegoat for our pain. With only enough margin of energy to survive for ourselves, caring for each other felt impossible.

Somehow, we saw it for what it was: grief infiltrating our relationship. Our pain caused us to be selfish and self-preserving, and it's hard to manage marriage without selfless love. Identifying it took effort and work. Since then, we've regularly revisited how our relationship has been impacted by grief. In a million moments of forgiveness, we've provided grace to one another for the different ways we grieve. We've withheld words and judgement—and asked for forgiveness when we didn't. Even years later, it continues to be hard. We are both very different people than we once were, and we're getting to know ourselves and each other again.

Even strong marriages can feel unsteady with the earthquake of grief, and rocky marriages may be on the verge of collapse. They don't have to. Instead, they can become stronger through communication, counseling, and a lot of time. While it takes vulnerability, selflessness, and dependence on God, it's worth the effort as the burden you share as husband and wife draws you closer together.

If you aren't married, or if you lost a spouse, you may find that similar selfishness arises in relationships with friends and family. It is hard to care for others when you can hardly care for yourself. It takes time and effort, but it is worth the fight. The vulnerability you can experience within these close relationships is difficult to manufacture outside of your times of deepest grief.

But he said to me, "My grace is sufficient for you,
for my power is made perfect in weakness."
Therefore I will boast all the more gladly of my weaknesses,
so that the power of Christ may rest upon me.
-2 Corinthians 12:9 (ESV)

REFLECT: How might you approach others with the grace you need yourself? Consider phrases you can repeat to yourself such as "She's doing the best she can," "He is acting out of his grief," or "She isn't the best version of herself right now."

Radical Forgiveness

Betsie and Corrie ten Boom lay in the barracks of their concentration camp. Their minds had almost grown accustomed to the fleas and smells. *What was life like before this?* With middle-aged bodies aching and groaning for nourishment, Betsie lay next to her sister as she told her of the dreams she had of coming back to this place after the war.

With her illness becoming worse with each day, Betsie gained a quiet exuberance as she spoke of rehabilitation and serving the people most affected by the camp's devastation—both the prisoners and the soldiers. She described the concentration camp with the barbed wire removed, the gray concrete walls painted a light green, and gardens planted all around. How healing the gardens would be! Betsie died just days later, but Corrie saw these projects come to fruition.[4]

While Corrie left the camp and her bodily suffering, she never quite re-entered normal life. *How could she?* While living through hell on earth, she experienced God's sustenance. Regular life fell flat compared to the heights and depths of her time at Ravensbrück Concentration Camp Instead, she traveled the world into her eighties, speaking about the goodness of God and forgiveness. Her full story is recounted in *The Hiding Place* and *Tramp for the Lord*, books that have greatly ministered to me.

Later in her life, Corrie finished a lecture about forgiveness and unexpectedly found herself face-to-face with one of her Nazi captors.

> And that's when I saw him, working his way forward against the others. One moment I saw the overcoat and the brown hat; the next, a blue uniform and a visored cap with its skull and crossbones.
>
> It came back with a rush: the huge room with its harsh overhead lights, the pathetic pile of dresses and shoes in the center of the floor, the shame of walking naked past this man. I could see my sister's frail form ahead of me, ribs sharp beneath the parchment skin. *Betsie, how thin you were!*
>
> Betsie and I had been arrested for concealing Jews in our home during the Nazi occupation of Holland; this man had been a

guard at Ravensbrück concentration camp where we were sent.

Now he was in front of me, hand thrust out: "A fine message, *fräulein*! How good it is to know that, as you say, all our sins are at the bottom of the sea!"

And I, who had spoken so glibly of forgiveness, fumbled in my pocketbook rather than take that hand. He would not remember me, of course–how could he remember one prisoner among those thousands of women?

But I remembered him and the leather crop swinging from his belt. It was the first time since my release that I had been face to face with one of my captors and my blood seemed to freeze.

"You mentioned Ravensbrück in your talk," he was saying. "I was a guard in there." No, he did not remember me.

"But since that time," he went on, "I have become a Christian. I know that God has forgiven me for the cruel things I did there, but I would like to hear it from your lips as well. *Fräulein*"–again the hand came out–"will you forgive me?"

And I stood there–I whose sins had every day to be forgiven–and could not. Betsie had died in that place–could he erase her slow terrible death simply for the asking?

It could not have been many seconds that he stood there, hand held out, but to me it seemed hours as I wrestled with the most difficult thing I had ever had to do.

For I had to do it–I knew that. The message that God forgives has a prior condition: that we forgive those who have injured us. "If you do not forgive men their trespasses," Jesus says, "neither will your Father in heaven forgive your trespasses."

I knew it not only as a commandment of God, but as a daily experience. Since the end of the war I had had a home in Holland for victims of Nazi brutality.

Those who were able to forgive their former enemies were able also to return to the outside world and rebuild their lives, no

Come Thou Fount of Every Blessing

Robert Robinson

Traditional American Melody

matter what the physical scars. Those who nursed their bitterness remained invalids. It was as simple and as horrible as that.

And still I stood there with the coldness clutching my heart. But forgiveness is not an emotion–I knew that too. Forgiveness is an act of the will, and the will can function regardless of the temperature of the heart.

"Jesus, help me!" I prayed silently. "I can lift my hand. I can do that much. You supply the feeling."

And so woodenly, mechanically, I thrust my hand into the one stretched out to me. And as I did, an incredible thing took place. The current started in my shoulder, raced down my arm, sprang into our joined hands. And then this healing warmth seemed to flood my whole being, bringing tears to my eyes.

"I forgive you, brother!" I cried. "With all my heart!"[5]

This story speaks more to me than any other modern-day example of forgiveness. She looked her darkest evil in the eye and forgave him, challenging me to consider the ways I need to forgive others. It humbles me to think of the grudges I hold tightly when there is an opportunity to release those strongholds.

The Bible has many examples of forgiveness, and I'd like to share two powerful illustrations. Allow the stories to move your emotions as you imagine the suffering, the guilt, the anger, and the strength God provided in these examples of radical forgiveness.

—

Jacob approached his brother. He'd brought gifts, hoping they would appease Esau's impending anger. Years ago, Jacob had stolen something of great value from his brother—the great honor and special privilege of the firstborn's birthright. Years had passed, and now Jacob, the deceiver, was meeting his brother face-to-face. Instead of a confrontation, Jacob was met by Esau's warm embrace.

"But Esau ran to meet Jacob and embraced him;
he threw his arms around his neck and kissed him. And they wept."
-Genesis 33:4 (NIV)

—

His body was pinned to a cross, beaten and bruised. Jesus was blameless and undeserving of this punishment, but He endured it. He was mocked, misunderstood, cast aside, and abandoned. He did not resist but accepted the path set before Him. Willingly, He was led to the slaughter, and as He was crucified, He prayed for His captors:

"Father, forgive them, for they know not what they do."
-Luke 23:34 (ESV)

REFLECT: Consider an example of radical forgiveness that you draw strength from. How does this challenge you?

Freedom in Forgiveness

It's exhausting to live in a world where we assume the worst of people. Threatened by their words, we put up walls and barriers. We fling accusations and allow our minds to fill in the gaps with a negative narrative about our circumstances and their role in hurting us. Truthfully, they may not deserve a second chance, but grace is simply that: undeserved.

> *"If you love those who love you, what benefit is that to you?*
> *For even sinners love those who love them...*
> *But love your enemies, and do good,*
> *and lend, expecting nothing in return,*
> *and your reward will be great,*
> *and you will be sons of the Most High,*
> *for he is kind to the ungrateful and the evil.*
> *Be merciful, even as your Father is merciful."*
> *-Luke 6:32, 35-36 (ESV)*

By choosing to withhold grace, we remain strapped to bitterness and further allow the hurt to damage our lives. Harboring resentment takes us captive in the darkest of ways. Hostility, bitterness, and judgement need not be ours to carry. As we release them, our soul is free to be filled with the Spirit of God and His fruit: love, joy, peace, patience, kindness, goodness, faithfulness, gentleness, and self-control (Galatians 5:22-23).

While forgiveness is difficult, it's not only something we do for others; it's something we do for ourselves. While extending grace doesn't come easily, you might consider some Creative Response to help work through these emotions and thoughts. By choosing to offer grace, we experience freedom.

From My Journal—After a difficult situation when I felt betrayed

I have grown in grace and forgiveness—a surprising amount— for [those who have furthered my hurt]. Life is much better when I assume the best of people, and then adjust and grow with understanding. There is a reason people act the way they do, and it helps to uncover it, discover it, and try to understand it. But it's hard work.

As you press toward the freedom of forgiveness, remember that it is a process. You'll still have difficult days in which anger, hurt, and accusations reemerge. Continue to work through them, allowing your heart to feel and your head to remind you of the Truth you know.

> "Forgiveness is an act of the will, and the will can function regardless of the temperature of the heart."
> —Corrie ten Boom[7]

REFLECT: Have you experienced freedom in forgiveness? Have you experienced the negative effects of bitterness and malice in your heart?

Creative Response:

Write a no-send letter expressing your feelings. This can be a helpful way to work through your emotions with others. This letter will explode with all your big feelings. You don't have to hold back. Share your hurts, frustration, and anger. When you're done, release this pain by burning the letter.

Take time to reflect and then write another letter. Take a walk. Pray. When you're ready, re-write the letter. Be a teacher. Explain why, and have the patience you would have with a child. Instead of blaming the person, consider that the death and grief are the root cause of your pain. If you're satisfied with the letter and feel it needs to be sent, go ahead and do so.

Art journal: Crayon resistant art. Use a light or white crayon to express words of truth. Paint over the words with a wash of dark watercolor paint and allow the truth to shine through the darkness.

Find and create your next Ebenezer Stone. As mentioned in the first chapter, building a collection of Ebenezer Stones can provide a physical reminder to you of God's help and deliverance. Look for your next stone today and label it with a paint marker. You can use a simple word, such as "grace," a phrase, or anything meaningful at this point in your process. Put it in a spot that will serve to remind you of God's presence and help.

Create a forgiveness box. Decorate the outside to show the peace of forgiveness. Put notes or letters inside to help release bitterness towards others, God, or even yourself.

Create a cross as symbol of the grace we receive. You could consider using wood, clay, or even sticks and twine. You may want to paint or decorate it, or leave it more rugged and bare. Consider mounting it on a canvas or hanging it on a wall or remind you of the forgiveness we receive in Jesus.

Capture your open hands. Trace your hands, use paint to create handprints, or use plaster-of-Paris to create a hand mold. This activity can remind you of the need to be open-handed to give and receive grace.

Five Minute Activity: Confession. Spend five minutes in silent confession. Grab a journal if you need more focus and concentration. Confess your

mistakes, your wayward heart, and your hardened spirit. Confess your ill feelings towards others, your hurtful words, and your attitude. Allow God to reveal other areas of confession. Allow His forgiveness to wash over you.

CHAPTER EIGHT

Courage

COMBAT FEARS, LIES, & THE ENEMY

The Enemy is Real

Alone in my dorm room in the middle of the night, darkness and deep-seated oppression swept over me. Lies heaped up. The core of my identity was shaken; my soul felt heavy and conflicted. Immediately aware this was a spiritual attack, I was terrified. Turning toward the mirror fixed on my wall, with tears streaming down my face, I spoke aloud angrily. My words weren't special, eloquent, or even memorable. I called out the darkness for what it was, telling the Enemy to flee again and again until the heaviness lifted. Deep rest fell on the room, allowing me to sleep peacefully until morning.

I'm sure it's not the only time I've had a spiritual attack, but it was one of the first times I was certain it wasn't just my thoughts or emotions. While I can't recall what led up to this moment, I'll never forget standing in front of the mirror and facing the lies of Satan.

The Enemy is real. He's not all that Hollywood or Dante's *Inferno* makes him out to be, but there are dark forces among us. We need not over-focus on this because God's perfect love casts out fear (1 John 4:18). However, we should live aware and prepared. We must recognize the power of the Enemy, so we can reduce his influence and defend against his attacks.

The Enemy's Intentions:

> The Enemy intends to steal what God plants, taking away God's words of truth (Mark 4:14-15). He sows lies and doubts in the places truth once grew.

> The Enemy tries to make us feel alone, separating us from the community God provided (Luke 22:31-32). In our loneliness, his influence is powerful, and our defenses are weak.

> The Enemy blocks the way of our path making us feel discouraged and incapable (1 Thessalonians 2:18). He paralyzes us with fear and doubt.

> The Enemy makes us question God's love, intention, and guidelines. He tempts us with a desire for full knowledge (Genesis 3:1-7). He causes us to stumble and hide, believing God cannot

forgive our sin.

The Enemy binds us and keeps us captive (Luke 13:16). He makes us believe we cannot be free, that we are destined to remain as slaves to him.

The Enemy fills our hearts with darkness, making us act selfishly (Acts 5:1-4). He intends to make us feel justified in our actions, even at the expense of others.

The Enemy has plans and intentions, but God can free us from Satan's oppression.

Be sober-minded; be watchful. Your adversary the devil prowls around like a roaring lion, seeking someone to devour. Resist him, firm in your faith, knowing that the same kinds of suffering are being experienced by your brotherhood throughout the world.

-1 Peter 5:8-9 (ESV)

In the sections ahead, we'll explore some common lies people experience in grief. As you read, you may find that you relate to some more than others. While they are referred to as lies, it doesn't mean the associated feelings are false; rather, it reveals that these feelings are not what God intended for our identity. These are the feelings the Enemy creates to keep us captive.

From my Journal: October 21, 2016—Two months after Winnie died

I feel I've been attacked with so many lies. Lies about my worth and value. Lies about my sin and blame. Discerning truth from lies is hard, especially when they feel as though they could be true. I've been told that I can't be used. I have trouble understanding if these words are coming from God, telling me "be still" and that I am not in a time to be used right now, as I have so much healing and growing to do. Or perhaps they are words of discouragement from the Enemy that I cannot be used, that I am too broken. Can I be used, even in this brokenness? I want to hope for that. I want to hope that God is using this time.

REFLECT: How is the Enemy influencing you?

The Lie of Envy

Theodore Roosevelt famously said, "Comparison is the thief of joy."[1] It's easy to let Satan grab a hold of our hearts with envy, convincing us that *others* possess what we deserve. *They* live an easier life. We'd finally be happy if we had what *they* have. These thoughts destroy us, damaging relationships and creating impossible expectations.

Every single person carries a burden—largely unspoken or misunderstood. We envy others' lives, unaware of the unique affliction they shoulder. Most of us are just holding on through a crisis, big or small.

The eating disorder, the sexual trauma, the affair, the shame, the addiction, the failures, the chronic pain, the unfulfilled dreams, the difficult job, the mental health problems, the physical problems, the hurting family members: no one I know is immune—however perfect life may seem.

Instead of allowing envy to sink in and grab hold, remind yourself that the people you are envious of are likely fighting an untold battle. Cling to this verse:

For each will have to bear his own load.
-Galatians 6:5 (ESV)

Your burden is heavy. You may stagger under the weight of the compounding burdens, misunderstood by those around you. While you can cast it on God, the burden-carrier (Matthew 11:30), allow me to gently remind you: envy in your heart *adds* to your burden rather than alleviating it. Surrender your envy and affliction to Him.

Since you are my rock and my fortress, for the sake of your name lead and guide me.
Keep me free from the trap that is set for me, for you are my refuge.
Into your hands I commit my spirit; deliver me, Lord, my faithful God.
-Psalm 31: 3-5 (NIV)

REFLECT: When do you struggle the most with envy? Do you need to limit time on social media or with certain people? How can you remind yourself that judging and cultivating envy will not ease your own suffering?

NO ONE EVER TOLD ME THAT
GRIEF FELT SO LIKE FEAR.

—C. S. LEWIS

The Lie of Uselessness

A crisis of identity followed Clive's death, and a deep questioning of value followed Winnie's death. I felt burdened by my deep grief, and I also felt burdensome to others. I was unable to keep my children alive, unable to work full time, and unable to be the sister, friend, daughter, or wife that I wanted to be.

The lie of uselessness cuts deeply, causing us to question our worth, purpose, and very identity. It's easy to compare ourselves to others or to our former self.

In these moments, we can consider our framework for defining value and purpose. A newborn's value isn't called into question even when they are helpless to do anything. Someone with a mental or physical disability still contributes to society, and we're all better for knowing and interacting with people of all abilities as we learn patience, witness joy, and see the world through a different lens. A stroke victim isn't blamed for an inability to eat or speak; a chemo patient isn't reprimanded for their hair falling out; a young child isn't blamed for not knowing how to read. All of them have value and purpose *just as they are.*

You are not a burden. You are a gift, even in your neediness. Your sadness and grief make you human. Your vulnerability connects you to other hurting people. Maybe in this moment you need to learn to be okay with your value not being in what you can produce, what you can give, or what you can contribute. You are valued and useful just as you are.

> *Be merciful to me, Lord, for I am in distress;*
> *my eyes grow weak with sorrow,*
> *my soul and body with grief.*
> *My life is consumed by anguish*
> *and my years by groaning;*
> *my strength fails because of my affliction,*
> *and my bones grow weak.*
> *-Psalm 31: 9-10 (NIV)*

REFLECT: How are you struggling with your identity or worth? How does God view you?

The Lie of Fear

It often arrives in unrecognizable whispers. The lie of fear is relentless in its control of you: Something bad will surely happen again. It will be too hard. They are judging me. I'll make a big mistake. It will always be this way. If you were prone to fear and anxiety before loss, it is exacerbated now.

After experiencing several losses in a short span of years, I began to expect death at every turn. Whenever I'd hear of a sickness or minor hospitalization, it mentally escalated into a scenario ending in loss. I would have described it as defeatism or cynicism but can now see that it was an anxiety of death and fear to hope.

Besides the big fears, my day-to-day life was filled with uneasiness. A normally sociable and go-with-the-flow person, I experienced a constant low-level anxiety that felt crippling.

I feared interactions. Social exchanges became strained as anxiety set in, and I could not always predict what would happen. *What if they said something hurtful? What if they said nothing?*

I feared changes. I needed to have a plan for everything I did. When things did not go as I expected, panic ensued. Changes felt disappointing and scary. *What if something else goes wrong?*

I feared decisions. *What if I made the wrong one?* Even a simple trip to the grocery store overwhelmed me by the potential interactions, the endless decisions, and the unpredictable nature of being in a public place. I wasn't carefree; I was a mess.

I was carrying unnecessary fear at all moments, failing to see God's provision. Similar to the Israelites' daily sustenance through daily manna rather than storehouses of food, God gives us grace to handle only our current needs, not future scenarios. I had a choice: fearing the future or taking one moment at a time. Choosing the latter, I trusted God to give me strength—and it's something I still have to do regularly.

I have learned to coach myself through these fears and prepare a response. *What if I make the wrong decision on groceries?* It will be okay. *What if the check-out*

At the timberline where the storms strike with the most fury, the sturdiest trees are found.
-Hudson Taylor

person asks about kids? I can get through it. *What if something unexpected happens?* I can make a new plan. *What if my worst fears become my reality?* God will give me the grace I need at the moment.

> *Because of all my enemies,*
> *I am the utter contempt of my neighbors*
> *and an object of dread to my closest friends—*
> *those who see me on the street flee from me.*
> *I am forgotten as though I were dead;*
> *I have become like broken pottery.*
> *But I trust in you, Lord;*
> *I say, "You are my God."*
> *-Psalm 31: 11-12, 14 (NIV)*

REFLECT: Write your deepest fears. Speak them aloud and give them to God. Allow God's presence to be your comfort. Speak His words aloud when your fears arise.

The Lie of Instability

Teetering on the edge, I wondered when I'd crack. *Am I too broken, too crazy, too far gone?*

In my grief, stories of mental health struggles began to interest me. Mary Todd Lincoln, wife of Honest Abe, was ridiculed for her hysteria and depression.[4] Often portrayed as unstable and needy, most people failed to consider the immense pain their family faced. Three of the four Lincoln boys died of various illnesses—at ages four, eleven, and eighteen—and their father was assassinated.[5] Her madness seemed rather appropriate.

These stories beckoned me in because I seemed so close to the realm of psychosis myself. While it's seldom discussed and could be unique to my journey, I suspect it's not. I felt too crazy and exceptionally needy to those in my life. While my struggles were acute and stemmed from specific circumstances, my compassion has grown for those who have lifelong mental and emotional health struggles.

Perhaps you can relate to some of my experiences: minor setbacks becoming major discouragements; inability to "bounce back" from small problems; a wandering and unfocused mind; difficulty completing tasks; mental and emotional exhaustion; a rollercoaster of emotions and moods with little predictability; deep depression; questioning my sanity and ability.

From My Journal: December 5, 2016—Four months after Winnie died

I'm teetering. I truly know THAT COULD BE ME. And maybe...that will be me.

I know there are 'right' ways to handle some of this—but do they really embrace the absolute CRAZY mess? The mess in my head? The fact that there are times I WANT TO RIP MY SKIN OFF because that's the way my heart feels.

I know I think about death more than I should. I consider the ways. I don't plan it. I'm not there. But the temptation is real. What if I'm too broken? Too broken to parent, to be used, to heal—and break again.

Most people who experience circumstances that affect their stability wonder: *Am I too far gone? Will I always be this unstable? God, why have you afflicted me in this way?* Even if you do not have clear answers to your questions, find comfort in knowing you are not alone in your struggle. Consider talking with friends, a bereavement group, or therapist. You may also find comfort from stories of other people who shared a similar struggle, such as John Piper's *The Hidden Smile of God* or Zach Eswine's *Spurgeon's Sorrows*.

Remember that while these feelings of instability are real and valid, they are a falsehood because they are not your true identity or where your value lies. The Enemy is trying to make you discouraged in every possible way. Grieving and processing will help you heal.

My times are in your hands;
deliver me from the hands of my enemies,
from those who pursue me.
Let your face shine on your servant;
save me in your unfailing love.
Let me not be put to shame, Lord,
for I have cried out to you.
-Psalm 31: 15-17 (NIV)

REFLECT: In a time of instability, what can you depend on? What can you cling to? What are your greatest fears in being unstable?

The Lie of Shame

My arms ached from emptiness, and my eyes fixed on the floor as I entered the church. Wishing to be invisible, I hoped no one would approach me. A desire to connect with God brought me there, but shallow interactions with His people felt painful. *Maybe we can just slip in and out. What are these feelings? Why do my eyes remain glued to my feet, the floor, the window, anything but the intimacy and vulnerability of eye contact with others?*

Why does church hurt so much?

Overwhelmed by intense feelings, Sunday afternoons became (and often still are) time for regrouping and resting. After church one day, I collapsed on the couch with Sam. As I fumbled through my words, I processed my emotions: it wasn't sadness, anger, or envy. While I'd experienced all of those feelings in my grief, this was one I had trouble pinpointing. Finally, I landed on it giving a name to my emotions: I was experiencing shame. The empty arms, the extra 20lbs of baby weight, and the inability to keep my own children alive all contributed to a sense of deep shame.

My shame hasn't completely gone away, but identifying it has helped me move forward. I'm able to process through my thoughts:

> *I feel ashamed, but the truth about it is I made the best decisions I could have at the time.*

> *I feel ashamed, but it's not my fault.*

> *I feel ashamed, but I don't have to carry that burden.*

Shame is a lie telling you it's your fault, you should have seen the signs, and you should have mentioned it when you noticed something. The Enemy uses shame to convince you that you're an outsider, you're unworthy, and you're undeserving. Shame says if you really loved them, you could have protected them. Shame makes us think we carry a unique burden that no one could ever understand. The Enemy tells us it's our fault, outcasts us from community, and replays the ways we could have done something—anything—differently.

This is a lie. It is not your fault. In my conversations with other grieving mothers, shame is a universal feeling—and one that is hardest to talk about.

GOD IS OUR
refuge
& strength,
A VERY PRESENT
help in trouble.
- PSALM 46:1 -

It's easier to express anger, envy, and fear because they're more understandable. Shame, however, is shoved into the deepest corners of our hearts, lingering and making us feel absolutely alone.

Give yourself the grace you need. Release your shame, and expose it for the lie that it is. Even if a mistake was made, God covers us with His grace and removes our shame.

Praise be to the Lord,
for he showed me the wonders of his love
when I was in a city under siege.
In my alarm I said,
"I am cut off from your sight!"
Yet you heard my cry for mercy
when I called to you for help.
-Psalm 31: 21-22 (NIV)

REFLECT: How has shame impacted you? How can you acknowledge the source of this shame and release the guilt you carry? What are some ways you can quickly bring truth to mind when shame comes on unexpectedly?

Discerning and Defending

As a city-dweller transplanted in small-town Illinois, I struggled with the lack of streetlights on my daily commute to teach. In the darkness of winter evenings, I'd make the 15 mile drive home along a winding highway, white knuckling the steering wheel. Oncoming cars' headlights briefly stunned me as I tried to keep my eyes focused on the road in front of me. In seven years and over 35,000 miles, I drove that highway in fog, rain, sleet, snow, darkness, and sunshine. The more I drove it, the better I knew it. The valleys and curves became easy to navigate. My eyes adjusted to the darkness and fog. What was once frightful and treacherous became a part of my every day.

My soul's journey has followed a similar trajectory. The first time I navigated grief, I felt completely lost—without a map, without someone to call on. While grief continues to surprise me, I've allowed the journey to teach me.

In my experience, it often seemed difficult to defend against Satan's attacks. Disheartened, I wondered how much I could withstand. In hindsight, I see the courage I possessed and strength God provided. God equipped me to counter the Enemy's attacks with the defenses of discernment, surrendering to God, abiding with the Spirit, and persevering past the darkness.

We can learn to recognize stealthy attacks by Satan. As the great manipulator, he wants us to reject God and question His goodness. In response, we must turn from the lies to the truth.

Lies:	Truth:
I'm a worse version of myself.	God is still working in me.
I'm unlovable.	I am loved, chosen, and adopted.
I deserved this.	The world is broken, not just me.
I have to hold it together.	In my weakness, God is strong.
I cannot show weakness.	I am created for community.
I'm a burden.	God desires to care for me.
Life is not worth living.	My story isn't over.

Where can I go from your Spirit?
Where can I flee from your presence?
If I go up to the heavens, you are there;
if I make my bed in the depths, you are there.
If I rise on the wings of the dawn,
if I settle on the far side of the sea,
even there your hand will guide me,
your right hand will hold me fast.
If I say, "Surely the darkness will hide me
and the light become night around me,"
even the darkness will not be dark to you;
the night will shine like the day,
for darkness is as light to you.
-Psalm 139:7-12

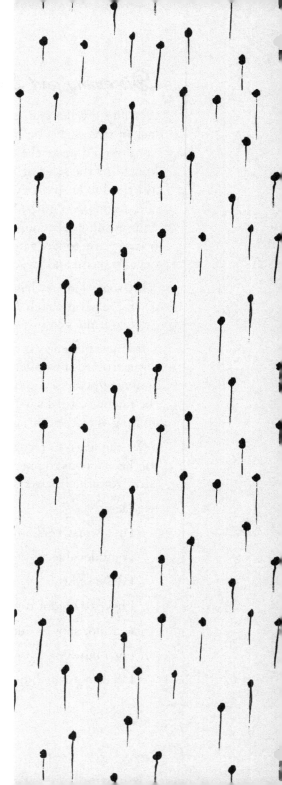

There is a stark contrast between Satan's voice and God's voice. In our trauma, grief, and darkness, though, it can feel confusing to discern the two voices. When God speaks to us from a place of love, care, concern, and grace, it brings encouragement. The Enemy knows nothing but discouragement. He tells us we will never get back up, we are useless, and we are unworthy. God's words will challenge and convict us, but they are rooted in love. They will refine us but not discourage us. Consider this lens as you try to discern truth and lies. In moments that are especially confusing, reach out to someone you trust to help you understand.

But when he, the Spirit of truth, comes,
he will guide you into all the truth.
He will not speak on his own;
he will speak only what he hears,
and he will tell you what is yet to come.
- John 16:13 (NIV)

REFLECT: What lies have you believed? Can you replace some of these thoughts with God's truth?

Defending by Surrendering

With an eager, childlike expectation, I tightly closed my eyes and asked God to reveal something new to me. My mind wandered and refocused, wandered and refocused, as the minutes ticked on. Slowly, an image began to form.

Against a fiery background, a warrior stepped forward. *What is this? Who is this?* I wondered. Arrows began to fire towards me, but the warrior's large shield blocked them as his body took a defensive stance, grounded and sure. *What are you showing me, God? I don't understand.*

Again, the warrior defended, raising his shield against an onslaught of arrows. *For the last two years I've felt alone and defenseless. I've felt unprotected, exposed, and even unloved. What does this mean?* As I took time to reflect on this image of God as my protector, I felt overwhelmed with understanding.

After Winnie died, I felt as if I had been left out in the wilderness alone to fend for myself. God seemed distant, as if He wasn't doing anything to protect me from darkness and the Enemy's attacks. Two years later, this image brought a deep-rooted sense that God was shielding me and that He had been protecting me all along. I was overwhelmed by the unseen battle for my marriage, my stability, and even my own life. Even though God did not spare Winnie's life, I know that He protected me from harm that could have resulted from her death. He fights for me—and you—and does not draw attention to Himself for doing so.

My eyes were open to see a glimpse of the great battle and I am humbled to think I considered myself unprotected and abandoned. I recognize that those feelings are still valid, even if they are inaccurate. It hurts to feel left in the wilderness exposed against the greatest harm. It's painful to realize that the One you trusted has done the unexpected. In these moments of great hurt, I must remind myself that the Evil One is set to destroy and bring calamity. God is fighting for me and protecting me from things I do not even know. He fights on my behalf. Although I do not understand, I trust Him.

I cannot, in my own strength, defend against the Enemy. I surrender, acknowledging that only God can fight this battle for me. I surrender my plan, my will, my weapons, and place my trust in Him. Surrendering isn't weakness but humbly admitting God is able when I am not.

None of this fazes us because Jesus loves us. I'm absolutely convinced that nothing—nothing living or dead, angelic or demonic, today or tomorrow, high or low, thinkable or unthinkable—absolutely nothing can get between us and God's love because of the way Jesus our Master has embraced us.
-Romans 8:39 (MSG)

REFLECT: What ways is God asking you to surrender to allow Him to fight for you? What might God be protecting you from?

When Across the Heart

When across the heart deep waves of sorrow
    Break, as on a dry and barren shore;
When hope glistens with no bright tomorrow
    And the storm seems forevermore.

When the cup of every earthly gladness
    Bears no taste of the life-giving stream;
And high hopes, as though to mock our sadness,
    Fade and die as in some restless dream.

Who will hush the weary Spirit's chiding?
    Who the aching void within will fill?
Who will whisper of a peace abiding,
    And each surging wave will calmly still?

Only he whose wounded heart was Broken
    With the bitter cross and thorny crown;
Whose dear love glad words of joy had spoken,
    Who his life for us laid meekly down.

Blessed healer, all our burdens lighten;
    Give us peace. Your own sweet peace we pray!
Keep us near you till the morn does brighten,
    and all the mists and shadows flee away.

Canterbury Hymnal, 1863

Defending by Abiding with the Spirit

What a beautiful thing that God has given His Spirit to abide with us, guiding us in every moment. On the good days and hard days, with each doubting step, in each moment of brokenness—He is there.

From My Journal: July 16, 2015—One month after Clive died

The courageous thing for me right now is trusting God and Him alone. It's not doing, it's being. God, give me courage to trust you. Give me faith to know you more.

From My Journal: May 1, 2016—Pregnant with Winnie

I know I'm not alone in this, but I feel so very alone. I feel discouraged and confused. Untrusting. Why is there such unrest and lack for peace? Where are you, God? Show me your presence. Show me your peace. Give me direction. You seem so far and uninvolved, uncaring. Do you care for your sheep? Do you know when they are lost?

Yet, I remember these verses:

I can never escape your spirit!
I can never get away from your presence!
If I go up to heaven, you are there;
If I go down to the grave, you are there.
If I ride by the wings of the morning,
if I dwell by the farthest oceans,
even there your hand will guide me,
and your strength will support me.
-Psalm 139:7-10 (NLT)

We can draw near to God as a defense against the Enemy's attacks. Abiding is a restful stance, not striving and burdensome. Still, abiding with the Spirit of God doesn't always come naturally, especially if you're prone to discouragement.

Practice abiding with the Holy Spirit by:

    slowing down to acknowledge His presence;

    breathing God in, breathing out malice and anxiety;

    listening to music that cultivates strength and rest in your soul;

    expressing our cares and concerns to God;

    writing out verses to encourage and re-center our souls.

Prayer is often challenging after losing a loved one. *Can I trust God? Does He care for me? Is there hope for healing?* We may not have words or strength to come before God in prayer, but we are not left alone or abandoned. When we can't pray, the Spirit intercedes for us:

> *Likewise the Spirit helps us in our weakness.*
> *For we do not know what to pray for as we ought,*
> *but the Spirit himself intercedes for us*
> *with groanings too deep for words.*
> -Romans 8:26 (ESV)

REFLECT: How can you abide with God throughout your day?

Persevering Past the Darkness

In the darkness of night, burdens seem unrelenting. Fears prevail; the minutes and hours drag on. Hope appears to be lost. Distractions fail, and we're left with a long night of perseverance—hovering over a hospital bed, sleepless with a raging fever, or in the throes of grief. Nights seem to carry a deep, heavy affliction. Night—whether literal or a dark night of the soul—often dredges up spiritual struggles. As the darkness creeps in, lies and fears are unleashed.

From My Journal: October 1, 2016—Two months after Winnie died

Yet, it's still so easy to feel alone. It's my unique burden, my unique journey. No one fully understands. I can't make them. They always say "you are not alone," but I struggle with that. Yes, I have companions, but in my head and in my soul, I journey only with the Father. And sometimes His presence feels far. Then I journey with the enemy. He tells me lies upon lies. Creeping in, confusing my thoughts. "Satan has no mercy," as Beth Moore said. Oh, so true. The attacks come, and I'm surprised. I shouldn't be. I'm the perfect subject. Wounded, broken, splayed out. Trying to crawl to shelter, but attacked by the talons and beak. He feasts on the almost crushed.

Why does God allow us to get to this point? I desperately want a hedge of protection. I want the refuge I've been reading about in the Psalms. But the storms whipped around me and almost prevailed against me.

We've all stumbled around in the darkness, looking for a light. God's light is given to us as a reminder of the truth. He is with us through the darkness. His light shines and reveals as He guides us through treacherous paths.

In him was life, and that life was the light of all mankind.
The light shines in the darkness,
and the darkness has not overcome it.
-John 1:4-5 (NIV)

The Lord is my light and my salvation—
whom shall I fear?
The Lord is the stronghold of my life—
of whom shall I be afraid?
-Psalm 27:1 (NIV)

His light gives us ability to persevere on the difficult road before us. This isn't done in our own strength and grit but in dependence upon Him. Instead of allowing the Enemy to attack us with lies—drumming up fear, envy, anxiety, shame and bitterness—we persevere in our faith. Perseverance isn't striving but purposefully stepping forward with God in the midst of a hard race.

We persevere by:

> praying away lies with truth;
>
> writing out verses to help dispel the Enemy's attack;
>
> depending on community that surrounds you;
>
> speaking truth aloud, preaching messages to yourself;
>
> turning away from things that destroy and returning to the light.

Some days an act of perseverance is as simple as getting out of bed to face the day. Allow God to give you strength and courage to do the next thing, keep getting back up, and keep moving forward.

REFLECT: Where do you need to let God's light shine? How is God asking you to persevere in your grief?

A Mighty Fortress Is Our God

Martin Luther

A migh-ty for-tress is_ our God, A bul-wark ne-ver fail - ing; Our
Did we in our_ own strength con-fide, Our stri-ving would be lo - sing; Were
And tho' this world, with de-vils filled, Should threa-ten to un-do_ us, We
That word a-bove_ all earth-ly pow'rs, No thanks to them, a-bi - deth; The

hel-per He,_ a - mid_ the flood Of mor-tal ills pre-vail - ing: For still our an-cient
not the right Man on_ our side, The Man of God's own choos - ing: Dost ask who that may
will not fear, for God_ hath willed His truth to tri-umph thro'_ us: The Prince of Dark-ness
Spi-rit and_ the gifts are ours Thro' Him who with us si - deth: Let goods and kin-dred

foe Doth seek to work us woe; His craft and pow'r are great, And,
be? Christ Je-sus, it is He; Lord Sa-ba-oth, His name, From
grim, We trem-ble not for him; His rage we can en-dure, For
go, This mor-tal life al-so; The bo-dy they may kill: God's

armed with cru-el hate, On earth is not his e - qual.
age to age the same, And He must win the bat - tle.
lo, his doom is sure, One lit-tle word shall fell_ him.
truth a-bi-deth still, His king-dom is for-e - ver.

Creative Response:

Find and create your next Ebenezer Stone. As mentioned in the last chapter, building a collection of Ebenezer Stones can provide a physical reminder to you of God's help and deliverance. Look for your next stone today and label it with a paint marker. You can use a simple word, such as "courage," a phrase, or anything meaningful at this point in your process. Put it in a spot that will serve to remind you of God's presence and help.

Practice discerning truths and lies. Make a column of lies followed by a column of truths to combat those lies. Preach the truth to yourself over and over. Allow the Spirit of God to give you discernment between the truth and lies.

Art Journal: Focus on Shelter. Psalm 91:2 says: "I will say of the Lord, 'He is my refuge and my fortress, my God, in whom I trust.'" Create an image of the shelter God provides for you as His child. Is it a wing, a building, a large tree? Where are you in the image?

Use collage to juxtapose light and darkness. Pick a few contrasting shades of paper. Rip or cut them, then glue them to create an image. As you form this image, what does God reveal to you?

Take photographs that play with light and shadows. You can catch rays of light, highlight the contrast between dark and light, capture the sunrise or sunset, and play with shadows or low-light settings.

Spend sleepless nights in scripture. Focus on God's truth by reading and speaking aloud verses that remind you of His presence and protection. Try starting with Psalm 16, Psalm 23, Psalm 84, or Psalm 91.

Remember you are a beloved child of God. Take some time to be still and allow God's truth to help you see your value as His child: needy, broken, and so dearly loved. Allow yourself to imagine what God sees when He looks at you and the compassion He holds for you as His child. Write down your thoughts and reflections.

Read old hymns. Focus particularly on parts of the hymns that mention darkness of the soul or persevering during the Enemy's attacks. What encouragement can you draw from these words? A few hymns you can start with: "My

Hope is Built on Nothing Less", "Turn Your Eyes Upon Jesus", "It is Well with My Soul", and "A Mighty Fortress is Our God".

Ask for prayer. In times of heaping lies and heavy darkness, it's been helpful to have someone pray over me. Asking for this doesn't come easily, but it helps silence the lies. Ask a friend or pastor to pray over you.

Five Minute Activity: Verse of boldness. Pick one verse that has given you strength and courage. Write the verse five times, increasing in size and boldness each time. Hang it somewhere you'll see it often.

CHAPTER NINE

Joy

TRANSFORMATION & RENEWAL

All Shall be Well

Standing by our front door, Sam hugged me and whispered, "It will be okay."

My body was stiff, hardened like my heart. Unable to will my arms to hug back, I mumbled. "I don't know if it will. I don't think it will."

Sam, the ever-reasonable one, was able to think further ahead than I. He drew comfort from eternal promises that day, as he wrote on our chalkboard:

> "All shall be well,
>
> and all shall be well,
>
> and all manner of things shall be well."
>
> - Lady Julian of Norwich[1]

Those words haven't changed from our hallway chalkboard in three years, but my heart has. That day, all I could see was my immediate future; all I could feel was the pain; all I could picture were two graves side-by-side.

But, slowly and miraculously, joy began to fill the cracks. I remembered the pure love experienced in the short days with Clive and Winnie, and my heart filled with gratitude. I opened my heart to the idea of adoption, and then opened it fully to a new baby. I opened my soul to God and prayer, to sorrow and lament. And slowly, a deep-seated soul joy released within, like a seed bursting forth. I'd almost missed it—this spring creeping in—the new growth in my soul and spirit. Life has moved forward with joy and sorrow intertwined.

Things aren't always happy in my day-to-day life. Grief still shocks me with its ability to pounce and topple me. But it's still a good life despite all the pain and sorrow. It's a life that has more depth and meaning because of the sorrow. And someday, in eternity, *all shall be well.*

As I write this chapter, it's winter. I'm writing by a window watching snow blow. Bare trees and gray skies extend as far as my eyes can see. It's dreary. No new growth is springing up, and the grass is a faded green under the scattered leaves and snow. Nature rests. And me? Spring and summer bring to mind joyful exuberance, but winter—*what joy is found here?*

It's a quiet joy, even when the tree doesn't grow, and the flowers don't bloom.

An unshakable joy, even when the cold wind blows harshly. A secret joy that no one can steal. A subtle joy that creeps in and changes the very way we live—even as we live in pain. *Where does this come from? Only the Lord. The joy of the Lord is my strength.*

> *But only the redeemed will walk there,*
> *and those the Lord has rescued will return.*
> *They will enter Zion with singing;*
> *everlasting joy will crown their heads.*
> *Gladness and joy will overtake them,*
> *and sorrow and sighing will flee away.*
> *-Isaiah 35:9-10 (NIV)*

It's okay not to be okay; a part of you will always be grieving and sad. Even still, you are free to come out from the shadows. You are free to emerge as a deeper, wiser, and transformed person. There is room for both sorrow and joy on these sad, hard, happy, beautiful days.

REFLECT: Are there times you felt as if joy was entirely absent and unattainable? How has joy crept in? What does this season look like?

NO SOUL THAT SERIOUSLY AND CONSTANTLY DESIRES JOY WILL EVER MISS IT. THOSE WHO SEEK FIND. TO THOSE WHO KNOCK IT IS OPENED.

—C. S. LEWIS

Heights and Depths

Free from the EEG wires and the nasal cannula that supplied her oxygen, all that remained were some monitoring wires and a feeding tube. We were stepping forward with hopeful progress.

I held Winnie close, soaking in what felt like the most normal experience in the world. Wires were unnoticeable; the hospital lights were dim. She was three days old, and her skin pressed against mine in the sticky warmth that only a newborn's does. Joy filled my heart as I held her closely, marveling at the sanctity of this moment, remembering her sweet brother's similar warm touch.

Her head nestled into me, and she was home.

> *Though the fig tree should not blossom,*
> *nor fruit be on the vines,*
> *the produce of the olive fail*
> *and the fields yield no food,*
> *the flock be cut off from the fold*
> *and there be no herd in the stalls,*
> *yet I will rejoice in the Lord;*
> *I will take joy in the God of my salvation.*
> *God, the Lord, is my strength;*
> *he makes my feet like the deer's;*
> *he makes me tread on my high places.*
> *-Habakkuk 3:17-19 (ESV)*

I have known love and joy in their purest forms. Deep sorrow has accompanied it, but it doesn't diminish the joy. Instead they intermingle, allowing me to experience a richer, fuller perspective. *Can we truly experience and understand the heights of joy and strength of love when things are only going well?*

If I had to do it again, I'd choose my life—each and every time. I'd choose Sam and Clive and Winnie and Corrie and all the accompanying pain. They are (and always will be) worth the pain because love is worth it.

So, if he wanted the heights of joy, he must have, if he could find it, a great love. But, in the books again, great joy through love seemed always to go hand in hand with frightful pain. Still, he thought, looking across the meadow, still the joy would be worth the pain—if indeed they went together. If there were a choice—and he suspected there was—a choice between, on the one hand, the height and depths and, on the other hand, some sort of safe, cautious middle way, he, for one, here and now chose the heights and depths.

Since then the years had gone by and he—had he not had what he chose that day in the meadow? He had had the love. And the joy—what joy it had been! And the sorrow. He had had—was having—all the sorrow there was. And yet, the joy was worth the pain. Even now he reaffirmed that long-past choice.

-Sheldon Vanauken, *A Severe Mercy*[3]

REFLECT: As you consider your heights and depths, what comes to mind? How does this excerpt help you process the joy and pain?

You turned my wailing into dancing;

you removed my sackcloth and clothed me with joy,

that my heart may sing your praises and not be silent.

Lord my God, I will praise you forever.

—*Psalm 30:11-12*

Those who
SOW WITH TEARS
will reap
WITH
Songs of Joy.
- PSALM 126:5 -

Transformed through Suffering

April 10, 2015, was my last day of normal. I wore a blue and green striped dress, brown leggings, and a belt just above my bump. It was the last day I went to work, smiled and rubbed my belly innocently, and went to my routine doctor's appointment.

While drinking the "dreaded" glucose test beverage, I thought of all the complaints I'd heard. *This isn't so bad*, I thought. *I mean, it doesn't taste good, but it's the least I can do to help care for my baby.* I felt grateful.

About an hour later, I was told, "I hear an irregular heartbeat. I'm going to call the hospital and have you admitted."

"Should I go home and get anything?" I asked.

"No, just call your husband. You need to go straight there."

"What about my glucose test?" I asked, hoping they could draw blood so I wouldn't have to repeat it at my next appointment.

"Let's not worry about that." I'm sure she wondered about my comprehension by this point. "Can you drive yourself to the hospital, or should I get an ambulance?"

Somehow I managed to call Sam and drive myself to the hospital in a daze. That night, as we settled into a hospital room and awaited testing, we named him Clive.

—

Everything in life is marked by time with these events: before Clive, after Clive, before Winnie, after Winnie. Before the hospitalization, after the hospitalization; before the diagnosis, after the diagnosis; before the heartbreaking news, after the heartbreaking news. Before death, after death.

I look back at pictures of us before our children died, photos with them, and photos of pregnancy, and it pains me. What JOY we had, what ignorant bliss. I wouldn't want the former me to know the pain that lay ahead, but it still hurts to see the innocence that was shattered.

Does it hurt?" asked the Rabbit.

"Sometimes," said the Skin Horse, for he was always truthful. "When you are Real you don't mind being hurt."

"Does it happen all at once, like being wound up," he asked, "or bit by bit?"

"It doesn't happen all at once," said the Skin Horse. "You become. It takes a long time. That's why it doesn't happen often to people who break easily, or have sharp edges, or who have to be carefully kept. Generally, by the time you are Real, most of your hair has been loved off, and your eyes drop out and you get loose in the joints and very shabby. But these things don't matter at all, because once you are Real you can't be ugly, except to people who don't understand."

- Margery Williams, *The Velveteen Rabbit*[4]

You are not the same. Your suffering has changed you. While parts of you may still feel more broken, all of you is more real. You become.

—

While I like to believe that I never expected an easy life, or that I never believed that good things come to responsible, kind people, suffering revealed my hidden thoughts and dangerous expectations. I watched others' suffering but never expected the immense suffering that lay ahead of me. Now, living in the aftermath, my perception of security is shattered, illusion of control is gone, and I am forever changed.

We exist in two realms: before suffering and after suffering. Our innocence is lost as we step over this great divide and find ourselves trying to reconcile who we were before and who we are after. We witness the ways grief has changed us—forever –and acknowledge the impact on our lives.

Our lives as we once knew them are destroyed, and we embark on a journey of transformation. We lament; we seek comfort; we protect our peace. We

Life only has meaning

if we have a

hope and a meaning

that suffering and death

cannot destroy.

—*Victor Frankl*

discover our identity as children of God—an identity that cannot be stripped from us. We wrestle with faith, begin to hope, and even forgive. We see the Enemy's plans and fight back with God's strength when ours fails. In all of this, we transform. Pain and suffering shape and grow us in ways we can't imagine. They deepen our souls as they break and rebuild us.

> *The desert and the parched land will be glad;*
> *the wilderness will rejoice and blossom.*
> *Like the crocus, it will burst into bloom;*
> *it will rejoice greatly and shout for joy.*
> *-Isaiah 35:1-2 (NIV)*

REFLECT: Can you recall one of the moments your life changed dramatically? How does it feel to look back on joy experienced before that moment?

Inexpressible and Glorious Joy

Days pass, blurred together. They are muted and gray, with a filter of sorrow cast over them. But then the joy breaks through—often through beauty and sensation: a song, an image, an interaction. The joy feels so high—such a break from the dreary land of grief. I know it won't be joyful and happy always, but these first glimpses of joy help me. They feel like a long-awaited breath, a reprieve from seriousness and sadness.

In the first year after the deaths of Clive and Winnie I struggled to maintain any steady sense of joy. My faith wavered; my emotions felt so unsteady. Now, years later, I can see the steady, quiet joy that is underneath. I carry the joy of memories and moments, the joy of knowing love. It's not exuberant, but it's brighter for the sorrow.

From My Journal: May 1, 2016—Pregnant with Winnie

I think there is pressure to move on and forward. Regain joy and happiness as immediately as possible. Therapize and medicate and self-care your way out of it. But truly in the suffering is where God meets us. Isn't that the thrust behind "I consider all loss for the sake of knowing Him"? Great loss can be great gain. And as much as I'd like to have Clive back, I've gained so much and I'm grateful for that.

Though you have not seen him, you love him; and even though you do not see him now, you believe in him and are filled with an inexpressible and glorious joy.
- 1 Peter 1:8 (NIV)

Inexpressible and glorious. I know my words will fail you in describing this joy, but God will not fail in His provision as you draw near to him. Continue pressing into Him, coming back to Him, and spending time talking with Him. While the joy and happiness that the world promises are mirages in the desert. Jesus can supply the deeply rooted joy for which your soul longs. Not circumstantial, but eternal, this joy cannot be stolen.

REFLECT: What are some glimpses of joy you've experienced lately?

Imagine yourself as a living house.
God comes in to rebuild that house.
At first, perhaps, you can understand what He is doing.
He is getting the drains right and stopping
the leaks in the roof and so on;
you knew that those jobs needed doing
and so you are not surprised.

But presently He starts knocking the house
about in a way that hurts abominably
and does not seem to make any sense.
What on earth is He up to?
The explanation is that He is building
quite a different house from the one
you thought of—throwing out a new wing here,
putting on an extra floor there,
running up towers, making courtyards.
You thought you were being made into
a decent little cottage: but He is building a palace.
He intends to come and live in it Himself.

—C. S. Lewis

Bitterness and Gratitude

I never knew I could be grateful for loss. Even now, those words fall flat and sound false.

I'm not grateful for sorrow, but in spite of it. I've gained a perspective that I would never have had otherwise. My eyes are open in gratitude to the world around me—the sun shining, the snow falling, the leaves shooting out from dead-looking tree branches, small moments of joy. I'm left with a choice between seeing the miracles surrounding my daily life or choosing to cling to the shadows. Holding space for beauty doesn't negate my pain, but it reveals a thought that many miss: joy and sorrow are intermingled, and I don't need to choose one alone.

From My Journal: October 2015—Four months after Clive died

In the moments I feel robbed from so many years with you, I remember all the sweet moments I had carrying you for 228 days and being by your side for 39 days. When I think of all the love and joy you brought (and still bring) me, I feel grateful. To be chosen as your mom, in all the world.

> *You have turned for me my mourning into dancing;*
> *you have loosed my sackcloth*
> *and clothed me with gladness,*
> *that my glory may sing your praise and not be silent.*
> *O Lord my God, I will give thanks to you forever!*
> *-Psalm 30:11-12 (ESV)*

> *So we do not lose heart. Though our outer self is wasting away,*
> *our inner self is being renewed day by day.*
> *For this light and momentary affliction is preparing for us*
> *an eternal weight of glory beyond all comparison,*
> *as we look not to things that are seen but to things that are unseen.*
> *For the things that are seen are transient, but the things that are unseen are eternal.*
> *-2 Corinthians 4:16-18*

As I sought help early in my grief, several resources indicated the choice we have between becoming bitter or becoming better. It wasn't something I could manage in my early grief, but as time passed I began to wonder. *Do I want to be a bitter and uglier version of myself? Or do I want to allow my life experiences—however hard—to transform me into a better person?* As I listened to the Spirit's guiding I was directed towards the light, toward healing, toward truth, toward forgiveness, and towards gratitude.

As I continue to choose between bitter and better, I consider: *What impact did my children make on my heart? What do I want my life to be known for? How can I be thankful for the life I am experiencing today?* When I'm open to gratitude—taking seriously the duty of delight and receiving the wonderful gifts before me—the light breaks in.

> "The brave who focus on all things good and all things beautiful
> and all things true, even in the small, who give thanks for it
> and discover joy even in the here and now, they are the change
> agents who bring fullest Light to all the world."
>
> -Ann Voskamp, *One Thousand Gifts*[7]

Healed people heal people, and hurt people hurt people. We are never fully healed on this side of heaven, but we want to move forward from bitterness, resentment, and darkness. If you find yourself consumed, it is important to acknowledge and understand the root of your bitterness and move towards healing.

REFLECT: How are you transforming from bitter to better? What can you be thankful for in this very moment? If you struggle with gratitude in the day-to-day, try writing one thing each day in your journal.

Joyful, Joyful, We Adore Thee

Henry van Dyke

Ludwig van Beethoven

Awakening to New Things

Ten days after our son died, my husband and I sat on a picnic bench at a quiet park. We were still trying to remain unseen by people. Clive had just been buried.

"I don't think I can keep my job," Sam said, unexpectedly. We walked through this conversation together as I gently reminded him of the great trauma and loss we had just experienced. Finally, although we acknowledged how profoundly changed we were, we agreed it was too soon to make a decision like this.

Over three years later, he finally left that job permanently with certainty that it was time. He changed too much to continue life in the way he had planned.

> *From My Journal: September 2016—One month after Winnie died*
>
> We were saying yesterday that this is all too big not to be used. We've been given great blessings, but such great burdens—and there is such a responsibility in that—in sharing it, journeying it, in doing something with this hard journey and hard story.

Clive and Winnie changed our trajectory. There hasn't been a clear and singular direction in our lives, and much of it has been nuanced and difficult to explain to others. We've had many small steps of obedience and tried to carve out moments to listen to God's direction as we move forward from deep lament into the ongoing mingling of joy and grief in our lives.

You might find you are so changed after loss that you must *do* something: donate money, start a foundation, write, create, make music, volunteer, or change jobs. There are new and beautiful things you can do as you remember your loved one. It may be as simple as setting out their favorite mug at Christmas, donating blankets to a hospital, or writing a note to tell someone you love them. Your experience has changed you, and it will continue to change you. Allow these changes to unfold with time, and relieve yourself of the expectation that you must accomplish something immediately.

I have spent too much time looking at what other people are doing and comparing my grief, capacity, and path to them. Some people start foundations, others change the medical field; some people host memorial 5Ks, others quietly remember; some people cry every day, others are numb.

It can be easy to feel like we are never doing enough to remember our loved one. Allow me to gently remind you that you are doing enough. This may look like getting up (or staying in bed) each day, facing (or hiding from) another holiday, going to work or school, or bravely (or barely) walking forward in life. Your changes will be different from others; your journey and timeline will be different, too.

Your path may change as time goes on, too. Just as it's okay to do things in memorial, it's okay to stop doing those things, too. It doesn't mean your love has decreased, but it may mean you want to hold it closer or express it differently.

I had many small steps along the way as I awakened to new things, including attending grief retreats, connecting with bereaved mothers online, and establishing a fund to donate children's Bibles to NICUs. We've hosted blood drives, had birthday parties for our babies in heaven, and hiked countless trails on the hard days in which we find ourselves broken and restless.

We've had plenty of tangible changes, as I've listed above, but the deeper, intangible changes are even more important—these are the motivations behind our actions. We carry changed hearts that are aware of suffering. We possess sensitive spirits and the ability to meet others with compassion and empathy. We're more willing to focus on things that matter and less concerned with things we "can't take with us." We've slowed down, strive less, and appreciate moments, art, and the beauty of the world in deeper ways.

There is a time for everything, and a season for every activity under the heavens:
a time to be born and a time to die, a time to plant and a time to uproot,
a time to kill and a time to heal, a time to tear down and a time to build,
a time to weep and a time to laugh, a time to mourn and a time to dance,
-Ecclesiastes 3:1-4

There is freedom in these seasons as we learn to live with sorrow and joy. We can weep and laugh, mourn and dance, tear down and rebuild. We're not betraying our loved ones as we move forward and awaken to new things.

REFLECT: As you read Ecclesiastes 3:1-4, what seasons do you find yourself in? What new things, purposes, and changes have awakened in you?

Creative Response:

Create a collage of a butterfly. Butterflies are a wonderful example of transformation. Use pieces of fabric and paper to create a butterfly collage. Starting with a printed outline or image of a butterfly may help with creating the shape.

Art journal—Thankfulness circles: Cut out circles and write prayers of thankfulness around and around within the circles. Fill each circle with words of gratitude.

Clay transformation: Create a bowl, nest, or another object from clay. The clay transforms under your touch, and working with your hands can be a powerful release for grief.

Consider special ways to celebrate birthdays and holidays. You might celebrate by preparing special food, donating gifts, spending time looking at photos or videos, or writing a letter. Making a list of ideas or plan in advance might help if you have difficulty with decisions. While there is no wrong way to celebrate, it is helpful to remember that even the best planned celebration will often fall short of what you'd rather have—the presence of the one you're missing. It is still worth remembering and celebrating!

Make cookies or a meal for someone. This is a simple and practical way to show you care and think of others. Write a little note to say you're thinking of them, too. Kindness to others in the midst of your pain is such a beautiful thing.

Use your compassion to help others. Consider raising funds for charity, organizing something to raise awareness, or getting involved in something. Be careful not to over-exert yourself, as your capacity is likely much lower, but don't be afraid to try something.

Find and create your next Ebenezer Stone. As mentioned in the first chapter, building a collection of Ebenezer Stones can provide a physical reminder to you of God's help and deliverance. Look for your next stone today, and label it with a paint marker. You can use a simple word, such as "joy," a phrase, or anything meaningful at this point in your process. Put it in a spot that will serve to remind you of God's presence and help.

Plant something. Either buy or grow something green. Allow this to help

remind you of your new joy growing even in the midst of pain.

Five Minute Activity: Gratitude Photo Album. Take pictures of things for which you're grateful. It could be as simple as a warm cup of tea or a beautiful flower. Start a "Gratitude Album" on your phone and add these photos to it regularly.

CHAPTER TEN

Your Story

PROCESS, WRITE, & EMBRACE YOUR STORY

Your Story is Not Over

I believe in the uniting power of stories. As we truly learn to see one another, we practice the art of empathy. By reminding us that beauty can come from brokenness, stories take off masks to make way for vulnerability, acceptance, and healing.

Your story is not over. It matters—the past pain and triumph, the untold pages to come. For as long as you live, you carry the pain, the healing, and the transformation of your story with you. You are the keeper of your story, as you choose with whom and when you share it.

My story isn't over. Clive and Winnie's stories are not over. And God's story isn't over. The beauty is unfolding, like green shoots popping through the ground after a long winter. I may not see full growth or understand the mystery on this side of heaven, but I can appreciate the beauty of the story even in the middle.

From My Journal: June 9, 2016—Pregnant with Winnie

Thank you, Lord, for answering prayers and opening my heart to see the way you do it. I've been so bitter, expecting only bad from you. Each new trial, however small, has felt as if you lack love and care for your children. But I was closing my eyes to the ways you do love and care. Thank you, Lord, for our intimate time with friends this week. To share in sorrow. I'd think that sharing sufferings would wear and drag us down, but instead it filled us with a sense of your work, your purpose, your story. Our role in that huge story unfolding. Thank you, Lord. The God of all comfort... who comforts us... that we may comfort others.

I have a huge gash across my lower abdomen, a reminder of Clive's entry into this world. It has healed over the years, but it will never disappear. I used to look at it with fear, as it brought difficult memories to mind. Now, I can look at it with appreciation—for the life of my sweet baby boy and beauty that took place with the pain. I see the healing, my body's remarkable way of restoring, reminding me of the healing that has occurred in my soul.

I HAVE LEARNED NOW THAT
WHILE THOSE WHO SPEAK
ABOUT ONE'S MISERIES USUALLY HURT,
THOSE WHO KEEP SILENT HURT MORE.

-C. S. LEWIS

Scars remind us of pain and suffering, but they also remind us of healing. Scars show our strength, resilience, and perseverance. Scars show God's miraculous work and grace in our lives. We can be unashamed of our scars; they tell His story.

As you work through your pain, scars, and healing, note your progress as it ebbs and flows. Your time spent reflecting upon and writing your story will aide in this process.

From My Journal: June 10, 2016—Pregnant with Winnie

Lord, let me trust and believe you are working for my good, for the good of all in your kingdom and story. Not just my little life. Like the story of Joseph, let me believe this: "It was not you who sent me here, but God." (Genesis 45:8, ESV)

The majority of this book was written in the messy middle of my story: after Clive's death, after Winnie's death, before our adoption, and before a healthy biological child is in our arms. It was important to me to wrestle and capture my grief before the story could be tied up with a bow, before the path of our future looked clear.

As I wrote and wrestled through my faith, I had to grow comfortable in the disordered chaos of it all. Even if hopes never come to fruition, even if my world came crashing down again, even if I lost it all. I longed to pen my thoughts, to be able to say He is enough, and to share my story before there was a "happy" ending in sight.

A few years ago, I read two books about life-long struggles, each sharing sweet redemptive endings. It's easier to read, easier to sell, and easier to handle. But not everyone receives that type of story. Some people don't get to have the kids they wish for, others watch every friend walk down the aisle while they remain single, and many will struggle with unrelenting, life-long illnesses. Our stories can still be beautiful even in the midst of it all.

Perhaps you're still there, too. Aren't we all in some way or another? I encourage you to wrestle with your faith and story even as it continues to unfold.

REFLECT: What glimpse do you have of your story unfolding? What scars do you carry? How can you embrace your story even in the messy middle of it all?

In a futile attempt to erase our past, we
deprive the community of our healing gift.
If we conceal our wounds out of fear and
shame, our inner darkness can neither be
illuminated nor become a light for others.
—*Brennan Manning*

God's Bigger Story

Out of the 6 billion people on the planet, each of whom God loves, I am only one. Out of thousands of years of human life, I have only thirty-something. I am fully known and fully loved by Him, but I am such a small piece of such a huge story.

My life matters, but it is a small note in a big song, a single letter in a huge book. It's a story that I cannot understand or grasp, but one that I am told is beautiful. My personal story—and yours—is part of a story that spans all of time and existence, a story that involves deep suffering and deep redemption. It is a story of sacrifice and love, of restoration and healing.

God is a storyteller, weaving our stories into His Story. He is working things together—even horrible, unspeakable suffering—to be part of this story. He is redeeming all the lost and broken parts and putting it together to be made whole and new again. We cannot see and understand but we know this: in His Story, hope prevails, love wins, and mercy triumphs. In His Story, the messy pieces fall into place. In His Story, everything that is sad, broken, and lost is redeemed. Everything wrong is made right.

This Master Storyteller is doing things you and I cannot imagine—gloriously crafting the best story ever told, one that appears to have the Enemy win, one that seems hopeless and confusing. When all hope is lost, the King returns. He wins.

For now we see in a mirror dimly, but then face to face.
Now I know in part; then I shall know fully, even as I have been fully known.
- 1 Corinthians 13:12 (ESV)

Someday when we look in the mirror we'll see the big picture. In my moments of deep hurt, I can't begin to grasp this, but I can have hope that someday there will be restoration. And there will be no more tears.

From My Journal: October 12, 2016—Two months after Winnie died

This time is sacred. It's sanctifying. We don't want to waste our grief or our story. Refine and prepare me for the road ahead. I ask for a restored joy from these absolute ashes.

REFLECT: Do you have glimpses of God's bigger story? If so, what are they?

Being Misunderstood

I've grown to accept the fact that I will be misunderstood by many people. Some people will see my vulnerability as an attention-seeking behavior; almost no one will understand my unique pain and trauma; others will focus on the fact that we have a living child and seem to be happy now, glossing over the pain in our past. I cannot fully express all of my experiences and emotions in an understandable way.

I will be misunderstood. I am misunderstood. Accepting that allows me to move forward with grace and a lighter spirit. It is not my burden to help people understand every part of my pain. My purpose is to point people to healing and truth. My story might be a part of that, and I have no control over the state of their heart and willingness to learn and transform.

You don't need to carry the burden of being misunderstood. You can accept that some people will not understand your complicated story, and you can move forward in the freedom of not having to explain it all.

There is One who knows and understands every detail of you—even the parts you do not fully understand yourself. He knows you more intimately than a spouse, parent, sibling, or best friend. He does not need clarification, justification, or explanation. He accepts you as you are and believes in who you will become.

REFLECT: How have you felt misunderstood in your grief? How can God meet you there?

Come & Hear,
AND I WILL
tell you
WHAT HE
has done
FOR MY SOUL.
- PSALM 66:16 -

Writing Your Story

Processing and writing your story is valuable work. As you write, you begin to see sentences and paragraphs of God's Story of the World. Sharing stories connects us to one another and to the Author, while freeing us from the tight hold that our trauma can have on our lives. As you write and share, you grow in understanding, kindness, and compassion.

As you begin forming your story, give yourself plenty of time and grace. It will be hard, worthwhile work, but it may exhaust you. Take your time with this process. Here are some helpful steps to assist you in crafting your story:

Make a timeline. Use several pages of paper to make a timeline of your life. While this could be a long process, it's a great way to provide the framework of seeing the bigger picture of your life and God's work in your life. It will look a bit messy and scattered as you go, but jot down notes and words as you draft this timeline.

Identify big events. These are the events and years that really impacted your life. Add to your timeline: changes, stressors, conflicts, moments of crisis, losses, sin struggles, major hurts, and great joys.

Identify losses and changes. For each major life change listed above, write down the associated (or secondary) losses or changes. For example, losing a job may have also contributed to loss of income, loss of identity, and changes in friendships and relationships with those co-workers. How did your life change? How did you change? How did your dreams change? How did your beliefs change?

Identify the impact on your faith. Each life change, stressor, event, or loss impacts your faith in some way. How did this negatively or positively affect your relationship with God and your faith? What did God show and teach? How was He still good and working? How did you feel hurt? What was the Enemy's role? How did the Enemy create lies, misconceptions, and steal trust?

Spend time in prayer. As you pray, release these burdens to God rather than trying to fix them. Thank Him for the blessings you have identified. Pray for wisdom to see the ways He is working your pain and hurts for purpose. Understand that working through these burdens may take time, and that is okay. Bringing your pain to God acknowledges your trust in Him and your desire to heal.

Identify people who have helped shape and change you. These could be people in any stage of your life. You can even consider including those you do not know personally, including authors, speakers, and pastors. What were the qualities of these people who you admired most? Do you have people like this in your life now? If so, how can you spend more time with them? If not, where can you find these people?

Identify the people who hurt you. As mentioned in the chapter about Grace, many people have hurt you in your life. How can you hand over these hurts to the Lord? How can you work through forgiveness and letting go of their control over your life?

Identify the joys of different stages of your life, including childhood and now. Each of us has interests and passions that are unique to us. What did you love to do? What were you great at? Who did you spend time with? What did you dream about your future?

Identify your unique gifts, skills, and personality. Each of us has unique wiring and capabilities. What are some of your gifts and skills? Consider taking a personality test (such as the Enneagram or Meyers-Briggs) and reading more about different personalities to gain understanding of yourself and others.

Identify where God has placed you. You could consider physical space, communities and subgroups, or friends and family who surround you. What circles has God put you in with friends and coworkers? What neighborhood does God have you living in right now? Who are the people God has placed in your life?

Take time to reflect. All of these components are pieces of your story. They all have purpose and have shaped you to become the person you are—for better or worse. As you look at your timeline and the answers to these questions, it may seem like a jumbled mess. Look for parts of your story that have shaped you the most. What do you want to learn and remember from these moments? Look for themes throughout your life, and explore those more. Perhaps you'll uncover a long-forgotten passion or purpose. Look for the small examples of faithfulness in your life and express gratitude.

Blessed Assurance

Fanny J. Crosby

Phoebe P. Knapp

Bless-ed as- sur- ance, Je- sus is mine! O what a fore- taste of glo- ry di-
Per- fect sub- mis- sion, per- fect de- light! Vi- sions of rap- ture now burst on my
Per- fect sub- mis- sion, all is at rest, I in my Sav- ior am hap- py and

vine! Heir of sal- va- tion, pur- chase of God, Born of His Spir- it, washed in His
sight; An- gels de- scend- ing bring from a- bove, Ech- oes of mer- cy, whis- pers of
blest; Watch- ing and wait- ing, look- ing a- bove, Filled with His good- ness, lost in His

blood. This is my sto- ry, this is my song, Prais- ing my Sav- ior all the day
love.
love.

long; This is my sto- ry, this is my song, Prais- ing my Sav- ior all the day long.

Start writing. When you are ready, try writing parts of your story. You can start by writing a short memory. You can write from joy or from pain, just get the words out onto paper or your computer. The act of writing will help you process, remember, and heal.

Share your story. As you feel ready, share with people in your life who will hold it with trust and reverence. Perhaps you'll share small parts of it, or perhaps you'll want to share it all. You can share in person, in a letter, in a blog, or in a small group. As you share, you may find others connect deeply with your path. You may bring healing to others, and you will certainly take steps forward in processing your own pain and triumph.

Always remember that your life has a purpose. Your story has meaning, and it is not over. It may not be linear or tidy, but it is beautiful as it unfolds before you. Press on, dear one. We're all still becoming.

CHAPTER ELEVEN

Our Story

A GLIMPSE INTO GOD'S BIG STORY

I THOUGHT I COULD DESCRIBE A STATE; MAKE A MAP OF SORROW. SORROW, HOWEVER, TURNS OUT TO BE NOT A STATE BUT A PROCESS. IT NEEDS NOT A MAP BUT A HISTORY, AND IF I DON'T STOP WRITING THAT HISTORY AT SOME QUITE ARBITRARY POINT, THERE'S NO REASON WHY I SHOULD EVER STOP. THERE IS SOMETHING NEW TO BE CHRONICLED EVERY DAY. GRIEF IS LIKE A LONG VALLEY, A WINDING VALLEY WHERE ANY BEND MAY REVEAL A TOTALLY NEW LANDSCAPE.
—C. S. LEWIS

I stand in disbelief at my story. Clive and Winnie seem distant, and I wonder if my life is still different, still impacted, still worthy of being their mom. One moment the fog is heavy—I struggle to know the day, month, or season; the next brings bring a refreshing clarity, remembering intricacies, smells, and the smallest moments that changed me.

The grief is still here—constantly, as an undercurrent—but it's changed with time. I've changed with time. My grief is less loud, less demanding, less needing of others' validation. I detailed the aftermath of my grief in this book, tracing my fumbling and sorting through death's rubble. And now, I'll share more of life's fullness and beauty, pain and triumph, crises and peace in our family's story.

We married—still practically kids at twenty-two and twenty-three—on a happy July day. "Bittersweet Symphony" played as we kissed and strolled down the aisle, and we began our life together.

We ushered ourselves into adulthood with responsibilities. A broken old home begged to be bought, and, ignoring the pet-stained wood and shattered toilet, we obliged. We functioned as a well-oiled machine: waking, reading, and eating together before leaving for work; traveling, volunteering, and fixing our home side-by-side; hosting small group, attending church, and watching movies on Friday nights.

Life remained relatively unchanged for five years as we planted ourselves firmly in our community. We paid off student debt and saved our money, taking a steady road before we felt ready to embark on our next adventure of growing a family.

Most of our friends conceived within a month (if not accidentally), so we waited until the "right" time. Then we waited, waited, waited. We'd lined everything up. *What was wrong?* Waited, waited, waited. Nearly a year later, we finally had a positive pregnancy test! My sisters, sister-in-law, and best friend were pregnant simultaneously with me, and after years of longing, life was changing.

A few weeks later, we experienced the pain and confusion of losing that baby in miscarriage. It couldn't have come at a more tumultuous time—in addition to our full time jobs, we were in the midst of opening a coffee shop in our community. Exhausted and overwhelmed by the coffee shop construction and the four appointments it took to confirm a non-viable pregnancy, we sank into grief. We struggled to maintain outward happiness for the new business while we were broken for the death of this tiny baby, long awaited and barely celebrated.

Grief came into my life with seismic quakes. Unable to slow down and process our loss, life became ugly as I grieved in isolation. This experience (and sharing about our miscarriage as a first blog post, months later) helped me understand how necessary it is to grieve within community. I need not hide my deep hurts. Vulnerability reveals the brokenness which unites us.

Bitterness and anger towards God grew. We had waited; we had done everything "right". *Why were we suffering? Why was everyone else's life so easy?* My heart slowly softened as I pressed into these questions, allowing God to comfort me as a child, and allowing His community to surround and love. We weren't alone in our suffering.

Half a year later, we witnessed the whooshing fetal heartbeat and movement of our second baby, marveling how the instant relief brought a happy sleepiness to the dark ultrasound room. We felt sure all would be well this time.

—

Before our gender revealing appointment, we rushed to Target to pick out two outfits: a blue suit, plaid bowtie, and a pink shirt; and a navy and white stripped dress with a yellow ribbon. "It's a boy!" we announced on social media that evening, with a photo of his outfit and ultrasound. With the chaos of working multiple jobs, the dress remained at the bottom of a storage crate in our entryway instead of being returned.

Our natural childbirth class gave us a weekly date night (complete with a trip to Sam's Club for the coffee shop), allowing time for dreaming, discussing names, and wondering how different our lives would be. We were excited to meet this boy—our son!—and prepared our home and lives to welcome him.

My 30 week appointment followed a normal day of teaching kindergarten. I waited for my doctor, sipping the sugary glucose test drink. As she listened to our baby's heartbeat on a Doppler, she became concerned at the fast rate and newly developed arrhythmia.

She sent me directly to the hospital where Sam met me. I checked myself in, still calm and naïve. Surely this was just a precaution; we would be home the next day. I didn't know two months later we would make the long drive home without a baby.

The hospital admittance brought a flurry of tests and specialists. A woman came in to do the echocardiogram in my hospital room. She wasn't wearing scrubs, her flowing top and jewelry indicating she'd been called in from a Friday night out. *Is it that serious?* I wondered. An amniocentesis came next with searing pain and pressure, as they searched for answers to the baby's supraventricular tachycardia (SVT or rapid heart rate).

The results to all the testing revealed a healthy baby in almost every way. His heart was structurally perfect, but its electrical circuits continually misfired to cause the rapid heart rate. "Treatable," we were told. They administered medicine—first through me and the placenta.

"He'll continue to take medicine after birth," they explained, "and he can have a laparoscopic ablation surgery when he's big enough." Treatable. That night, as we shared our prayer requests with family and friends, we named him Clive—a tribute to one of our favorite authors, Clive Staples (C. S.) Lewis.

After two weeks of constant monitoring at the hospital, they decided to transfer me to Peoria, where Clive could be admitted to the Children's Hospital of Illinois. I hadn't cried yet, even when one doctor gave me full permission to express my anger, but my throat constricted and eyes burned as they told me about the transfer. I became overwhelmed by the thought of making new connections with a different staff in an unknown hospital two hours away from home. But even more, we were headed to the hospital where our friends' five-year-old son Thao died just three years before.

Constant fetal monitoring and bedrest continued at the new hospital. The monitors on my stomach—which were error prone and troublesome to the nurses—irritated my sensitive skin, but as we listened we learned the rhythm of Clive's heart rate, its skips and beats, whooshing and rumbling as he moved. Anticipation built as we waited for our son to join us.

Clive was born at 32 weeks gestation, on April 29, 2015, when the doctors decided to treat his heart outside of my body. His tiny body had taken on nearly a liter of fluid as his heart struggled to work (hydrops), and he weighed a large 4 pounds, 14 ounces for his age. We already loved him, but our love grew at the sight of him—we remained blissfully unaware of how sick he was at birth until we looked back at pictures later.

After the tumultuous first few days of Clive's life, we had three weeks with wonderful progress and memories. The staff became family, caring for us as we cared for him. Friends and family surrounded us with love, prayers, and food. Photos and videos capture the moments I hold in my heart: his first clothes, his first bottle, skin-to-skin holdings. Clive's remarkable joy is what I remember most—his ability to calm our worries with his gummy grin and steady gaze. *How could a premature newborn know my soul's deepest needs?*

On several occasions, we stood at Clive's bedside all night as staff administered adenosine again and again to stop and restart his heart. Terror flashed in his eye for these brief moments, and we comforted him in the only ways we could—gentle squeezing of his hands and rubbing of his head. His cardiologists tinkered with dosages and medications but could not stop his persistent SVT. They told us it was uncharted territory. Yet when we interacted with him, catching his gaze and huge grin, he gave us joy and peace and hope.

We were on holy ground, in Room 338, as we shared glorious memories of a family: just a couple of parents loving, reading, snuggling, and changing diapers. The monitors, medicine and alarms became dismissible in the moments we focused on Clive and our love for him. Sometimes love breaks through the chaos, rendering peace.

One particularly hopeful day, we left the hospital and lay in the green grass, dreaming of the day we'd bring Clive outside. The seasons changed around us, but the hospital held no seasonal rhythm; the controlled temperatures and blaring lights contributed to confusion of days, times, and hours. God often reveals himself in nature, and His presence was evident in the warmth of sunshine on that spring afternoon. Out in the grass, hope was alive.

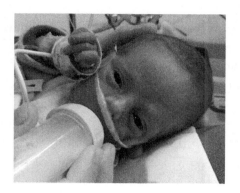

We got the call the morning Sam planned to go back to work. "Come quickly," they said. He turned around at the first exit and headed back, picking me up on the way. *We weren't there.* For weeks we rarely left his side, but—given his progress with oxygen and feedings—we'd slept away from the hospital. *Why weren't we there?*

Clive crashed in the early morning hours, his body cold and his heart rate slow. The medicine had overwhelmed his system, or the SVT had overworked his heart.

The room felt small and cramped when we arrived. *Was it the same room?* Clive looked perfectly peaceful but remained unresponsive. "We need to do emergency surgery. Do we have your consent? Would you like to hold him first?" I slid into the chair next to the isolette. "I'm not getting a heart rate," one doctor noted. With no time to hold him before they ushered him off, we remained in Room 338 after the flurry of staff left with our boy.

Our parents and pastor waited with us all day as they worked on him. I was handed Gatorade and vending machine snacks while my one-month-old was on an operating table somewhere in the hospital. Doctors came out to give updates, and we eventually heard he survived the surgery, but his heart only beat correctly with the aid of an external pacemaker. The cardiac arrest badly damaged his organs, but it was too soon to know the lasting effects. He was placed on an ECMO (life support) machine to do the work for his heart and lungs. My heart sank at the news—I'd heard of ECMO once before, when Thao was in the same hospital.

The life-sustaining machine was too large for the NICU, and we moved to the Pediatric ICU—in the same room Thao and our dear friends had occupied three years earlier. Our dark and calm NICU room was exchanged for a busy room with blaring lights, wide-open on one side to allow emergent access. An unfamiliar staff lingered at the nurse's station directly across from our room, often chatting about their everyday lives and problems. We felt exposed.

Clive's body was on tall platform bed, tubes and wires came out of his chest like something from *The Matrix*. It didn't stop all night long, the bleeding and swelling. He became unrecognizable—my baby boy—as he was laid out, chest still open for the machines to do the job his body could not do, his heart fluttering under a thin membrane.

Our moms slept in the waiting room; we were unwilling to let them see the horror we witnessed. Clive miraculously made it through the night, and the bleeding stopped. We met several new doctors as they came to tell us of the damage sustained by every organ. The long days of "wait and see" began.

His outcome looked bleak, but we had to maintain hope to survive. A nurse saw my desperation and told me, "Don't give up hope. He needs you to be strong." I stood on a wooden box next to his high platform-bed and held his hand, stroked his hair, and sang lullaby after lullaby, awing over his gentle squeeze of my hand, watching for his dark blue eyes to flutter open—attempting to put a lifetime of memories into a few days.

We continued the rollercoaster of hospital life—full of small progress and major setbacks—updating friends and family on Facebook, frustrated by their optimism and ability to only hear our positive words on the most desperate days. We shared hospital meals and slept in the room with Clive, fueled by coconut Cliff Bars and canned Starbucks Double Shots. Cards and pictures decorated the walls, poster-size photos of Clive hung prominently to remind ourselves of him at his best and to show the unfamiliar staff this little boy was more than tubes and ECMO.

For ten days we rarely left the room, waiting for updates from doctors and

Make our
SONS LIKE STURDY
Oak Trees,
OUR DAUGHTERS AS
Fields of Wildflowers.
- PSALM 144:12 -

nurses, waiting for rounds, waiting for movement. Our large window overlooked on a balcony garden and I watched purple Seuss-like flowers (allium, I learned when I planted dozens of bulbs that fall) bloom while my baby boy's life slowly faded. We snuck out to the garden for a few moments, desperate for peace, respite, relief.

Miraculously, peace emerged. The raw brokenness removed us from everyday moments and brought us back to the only source of love, comfort, and truth—Jesus. The nearness we experienced to God in those days was a gift. Somehow, within Room 423's walls, however harsh and uninviting, our faith remained steadfast and firm. With nothing we could do, little to offer, and no strength of our own, we surrendered—trusting God to take control when we had no other choice. It wasn't an active push of faith or bravely choosing hope in the midst of the storm; it was a surrender to the inability to muster up anything ourselves.

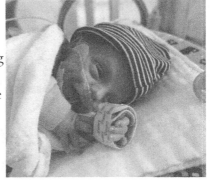

As the days passed, Clive's tender hands and feet turned black and blue due to lack of circulation, and he sustained a chemical burn from TPN leaking through his PICC line. *Is there any mercy?* His auburn hair remained untouched. Then, a day came of probes glued to his head to monitor brain activity. We drew a line: no, they couldn't shave his hair to remove the glue. The next day I picked the glue out, grateful for the opportunity to care for him in this small way.

His organs shut down; he stopped creating blood. Coolers with plasma, platelets, and blood—marked A positive—graced the room. *Is there any mercy?* I continued a daily list in my journal, recording the day's progress and prayers. I was crying for a miracle, pleading for healing, meanwhile, begging for mercy—in one form or another.

After 39 days with us, Clive Samuel died in our arms on June 6, 2015. We sang to him, released him from his broken body, and ushered him into the arms of Jesus. A holy peace surrounded as we let him go, knowing he experienced full healing in heaven, trusting we would see him again someday. Later that week, friends and family joined us to celebrate Clive's life and worship a God who is *still good* even when we don't understand His ways.

—

In the year Clive died, I became a student of suffering. Desiring to grow and glean from my pain, I read books, I wrestled with God, and I sought the truth in scripture. I held Clive's memory alive, close to my heart. I desired to grieve well, learning from those who went before me and pressing into intimacy with God.

Over time, the outline for this book was revealed to me, showing the healing nature of processing through creative expression coupled with God's word. I filled journal after journal with thoughts and prayers. Joy wasn't restored, but I caught glimpses of the beauty of life, even in the brokenness.

Six months after Clive died, we were thrilled to be expecting again. The high-risk pregnancy merited extra scans and monitoring to assure us everything was progressing normally. After finding out the gender, we named her after her great-grandma Winona. I rediscovered the outfit we had bought over a year ago: the tiny striped dress with a yellow ribbon.

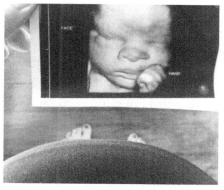

The pregnancy was full of bonding, and I was grateful for my side-kick during gardening and exercising, a constant companion on lonely days. We showered Winnie with love, affection, and prayers. Friends and family joined us as we anxiously awaited the arrival of this long-expected rainbow baby.

Everything looked routine in Winnie's pregnancy until the 30th week, when the doctors noticed fluid in her brain. As we continued to track it via ultrasound, they warned us of potential special needs but mentioned it could resolve by birth. Raising a child with special needs wasn't a concern for us, but we feared for her life.

In the midst of this, we experienced peace and a promise that this journey was a "new song." Winnie's verse became Psalm 139: 13-14 (NIV):

For you created my inmost being;
you knit me together in my mother's womb.
I praise you because I am fearfully and wonderfully made;
your works are wonderful,
I know that full well.

Our miracle baby was on her way, and we felt assured again and again (even from God) that everything would be okay.

At 38 weeks large, but rather small, they told me it was time. The placenta's flow slowed, and delivery day arrived. We packed bags and hopped into the car with car-seat installed. I glanced into the car's baby-mirror, knowing she'd be looking back at me in a few days as we took her home.

My body wasn't ready, so we induced, and a long wait began. We walked, bounced, danced with baby. For hours and hours my body tried to make sense of the contractions but couldn't relax enough to get there. A printed card hung in my room, sharing a photo of Clive and a snippet of our story, sharing what we desired from our birth and why, and sharing our appreciation for the hospital staff.

Winnie was born the next night, on August 12, 2016. *How long was labor? When was I induced? What time was she born?* So many details are forgotten.

But I will never forget holding her for the first time. Wrapped up in a blanket, her dark eyes met mine. My heart swelled with love for this miracle, for her and Clive, for the gift of holding her after birth.

She was safely here. Her birth was healing. Even as they voiced concerns and took her to the NICU to check things out, I felt an incredible peace.

We didn't anticipate a hospital stay. We didn't want one, so we didn't plan for one. *She's just measuring small during pregnancy; she'll be fine.* But even as the NICU stay became necessary after delivery, we assured ourselves it would just be a couple days.

That night, as I went to a separate recovery room without my baby or husband, I found myself relieved and proud. Even as I pumped before my baby suckled, even as Sam followed her to the NICU, even as many things felt eerily similar to the previous year, my face couldn't hold back a smile. Winnie Joy brought joy.

We navigated NICU life with ease, even in a different hospital. Quickly learning the rules and routines, we made a little home in the open-layout's cubicle rooms. Unlike the hospital Clive was at in Peoria, we couldn't spend the night with Winnie, but we watched via hospital webcam as she rested peacefully.

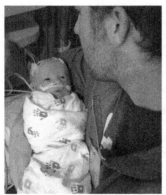 As we met with Winnie's NICU doctors, a geneticist, and her neurologist, they shared that there was potential for long-term developmental delays but no immediate concerns. Our sweet little girl needed so much from us, and we couldn't wait to give it to her. I made lists of prayers and praises each day in my journal, tracking her progress and celebrating answered prayers.

We held her each day; an MRI and EEG revealed good news; seizures stopped with medicine; and they fit a Pavlik harness to help her hips develop properly. A doctor deemed her eyes 'unremarkable'—his way of saying fine—which ruled out a condition we feared the most. They did a scan of her heart, precautionary because of Clive's heart condition, and found no heart problems. We worked on oxygen levels and feedings daily, eager to get her home.

There was serenity in the chaos of hospital life as I held her close to my chest. Her head tucked high on my collarbone, I couldn't see her well, but I drank her in—never knowing these moments would be some of the only ones we shared skin-to-skin.

Twice, I've been discharged before my baby. Twice, my aching post-partum body has stood, holding vigil over my children's beds for hours just trying to be near them. Twice, I've hated the breast pump that took my time away from holding their hands. But, twice, I've marveled at tiny features; twice, I've found a nasal cannula endearing; twice, I've thanked God for the gift of my miracle babies.

One day that week, we snuck outside in need of a break from the hospital.

Grabbing pillows and blankets, we walked to the park across the street and lay in the August sunshine, letting our skin warm from the over-air-conditioned hospital. We recalled our grassy nap when Clive was doing well, and we were thankful for Winnie's progress.

By Friday, at one week old she no longer needed the phototherapy lights for bilirubin levels—allowing for more time in our arms and the removal of her eye mask. Saturday, the nurses dressed her and moved her to a crib for the first time, showing her ability to regulate her body temperature.

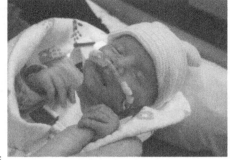

We had the best day with her, with the semi-privacy of the NICU curtain we shut out the other families and babies and celebrated with one another—holding, snuggling, and snapping pictures. Winnie's sweet frame was tiny, her fingers long and thin like Aunt Holly's, her brow furrowed, her skin soft. She was peaceful and restful in our arms, knowing it was where she belonged.

We left for dinner, returning to check on her later that night. My face beamed with joy and pride in her progress to a crib. She was resting peacefully in her bed. We held her again and said goodnight.

As we walked away from the hospital, I remember telling Sam something worried me. I couldn't shake the feeling she'd be cold in her crib, that she'd be alone, that something might happen. He reassured me as he always does.

—

A middle of the night pumping session had me awake when Sam's phone rang; the ringtone is burned in my mind. He started dressing as he replied "We'll be right there." I asked questions as we grabbed keys and phones. "What did they say? What was the tone?" "They had to intubate her. They said to come quickly." Our experience told us this was serious.

We ran across the street to the hospital, trying two locked entrances as we

Never be afraid to trust

an unknown future

to a known God.

—*Corrie ten Boom*

circled around the building, finally entering through the ER. We backtracked through the hospital, frustrated by slow elevators and long hallways. As we were ushered in by NICU nurses, our 9-day-old baby lay on a tall platform bed, surrounded by a team. Chest compressions, oxygen, shouting—everything indicated last life-saving measures.

I didn't fight my way over to her. We both sank into nearby chairs and watched in silence. If there was any chance she could survive, I didn't want to get in the way. Later, I'd recall these moments with frustration. *Why didn't I scream? Why didn't I break down? A mom should have loud, anguishing wails for her dying child, right?*

I covered my face with my hands, shaking my head. This can't be happening. This can't be happening again. Tears didn't come. My own heart and lungs struggled to go on, feeling as if the life was being pulled from my body. I prayed I might be taken instead. *Spare her, God.*

The night shift doctor crouched by our chairs. We'd never met the man who delivered the news: "I'm sorry."

We asked some questions, and he gave some speculative answers, later confirmed with the autopsy: Her heart's ductus had closed, as a normal newborn's does, but her aorta had an undetected constricted coarctation that stopped necessary blood flow. They had administered the emergency medicine too late, rendering surgery impossible. It was undetected by the scans of her heart and would have been treatable.

The team stepped back at last, efforts exhausted. With a deafening silence, they walked away, and we approached Winnie's body laying lifeless. "I want to hold her. I want these tubes out now." A nurse told me she'd have to inquire. "Sometimes they affect the autopsy. I'll see what we can do." Even after her death, I remained powerless. The doctor obliged, and they removed the tubes from her perfect form.

I sat and held her, the thin NICU curtain separating us from the other babies. Mercifully, we moved to a private room in another wing, Winnie's body transported under a white sheet beside us, where we held her and allowed family to come say hello and goodbye. A favorite nurse began her shift with us, offering great care and compassion as she took footprints, handprints, and made plaster forms. We tenderly bathed Winnie and changed her into pajamas, swaddling her tight.

The sun rose over the adjacent hospital building while we were in that private room. I desired to snuff it out, wanting the darkness of night to remain. I resented the new day, time moving forward without her.

We left her body at the hospital a couple hours later—one of the hardest moments of my life. Sam and I drove home together, listening to the lament by the Brilliance:

> Oh God, have you forsaken me?
>
> Forsaken me, forsaken me
>
> Oh God, have you forsaken me?
>
> Forsaken me, forsaken me

We sat and watched *Les Misérables* that day, unable to find anything else to touch the pain in our hearts. The young funeral director called and accidentally started the conversation with "How are you doing today?" (twice). "Not good," I muttered back, "My daughter just died." We came home to a nursery ready for a baby girl, and we planned her funeral.

It became a busy week, coordinating and throwing myself into the work of planning. This was the only celebration she'd ever get—no birthdays, no wedding. Though my pain was insurmountable, she deserved a beautiful service, not one filled only with tears and sorrow. We made a video, poured over photos, printed pictures, ordered wildflower seeds, picked songs and verses, and sketched a flower for her headstone's illustration. Pouring love out for her came easily because there was so much love to give.

Winnie was buried on her due date, August 26, 2016. They lay her tiny body in a tiny hole next to her brother's grave. Our dear friends learned and played songs for her service—a beautiful lament. I don't remember everything, but I remember celebrating her well.

At one time, I couldn't remember the happy parts of Winnie's life. Her absence loomed larger and darker than the brief week we had her in our arms. Time—and careful processing—has allowed me to focus on the qualities of my daughter I never wish to forget:

> *Her peace.* Winnie's demeanor was full of peace and rest. She seldom fussed or squirmed. I am still humbled by this quality, still

learning from her.

Her value. As a newborn, her contribution to society was insignificant. She required care, even needed additional support. But—her value was innately given, by God, and did not change or diminish depending on what she could contribute or accomplish.

—

With all their similarities, Clive and Winnie's deaths were incredibly different to us. Clive's felt merciful at the end of his challenging heart problems and pain he endured. Sweet Winnie was ripped away from our arms with no warning and no understanding.

Our processing of their deaths has been very different, too. Winnie's death has rocked our faith to its core. It's shattered us, and reshaped us, and we're still figuring it out. Clive's death gave me words and ratified my faith, Winnie's death brought loneliness and confusion.

Clive was buried in that little suit with a pink shirt; Winnie was buried in that navy dress with the little yellow ribbon. Even with extensive genetic testing, doctors continue to see no connection in their deaths. Even with a clear answer, it wouldn't be an answer enough. We don't understand, and we suspect we never will in this life. But, in the moments when a friend's life crumbles, and she calls for care and support, I see a glimpse of why I have been a student of suffering.

—

Not long after Winnie died, we decided to pursue adoption. Our desire for a child to raise had only grown as we loved and lost, loved and lost. While still deep in grief, the adoption process began a few months later with classes and books, a home-study, and an adoption profile. Along the way, we experienced a failed match and found ourselves devastated and unprotected again.

When a birthmother contacted us just six weeks before her delivery, we stepped forward with caution and very weary hearts. Coralie Marie entered the world on July 20, 2017—a full nine months after we started the adoption process—and entered our arms just minutes later. She felt like home as we cradled and rocked her in our local hospital.

Although we experienced complications along the way, we adopted Corrie as a newborn and finalized the adoption several months later. Her namesake is Corrie ten Boom, a holocaust survivor whose faith sustained her through unspeakable horrors. We maintain a positive relationship with Corrie's birthmother, who loves and bravely chose life for her child.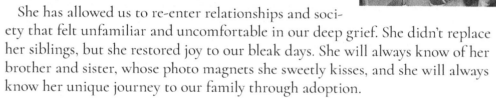

Corrie is a spunky and happy child, full of entertainment and able to do a host of facial expressions on command. Her adoration of nature and people (and carbs) fits perfectly into our family, and she's the perfect addition. Watching her grow is a gift we seldom take for granted.

She has allowed us to re-enter relationships and society that felt unfamiliar and uncomfortable in our deep grief. She didn't replace her siblings, but she restored joy to our bleak days. She will always know of her brother and sister, whose photo magnets she sweetly kisses, and she will always know her unique journey to our family through adoption.

—

In the months before this book was published, we learned we were expecting another baby—a sweet boy we've named Miles Dietrich. While everything is progressing normally as we quickly approach my due date, the future remains unclear. Yet, we are choosing to walk in hope. Fear knocks on my door daily, but I remind myself that if I let fear win I would have never known the love of my family. Afraid of pain, I'd have closed my heart to the possibilities before me. I'd have missed Sam and Clive, and I'd certainly have lost the opportunity to know Winnie and Corrie—and this baby boy that is kicking as I write. Fear steals. But there is no fear in love, and perfect love casts out fear (1 John 4:18).

It's a constant battle against fear, one that has me up for hours most nights, one that brings anxiety and nightmares. But love—true love!—and life—true life!—is worth the pain. Heights and depths, joy and pain. Once more, we remain open-handed and vulnerable as we wait. Our hearts are opening in love for this new blessing.

And here we are: still struggling, still healing, still living in mystery. Grief impacts our parenting and marriage, stirring up bitterness and brokenness; other moments, our hands lift open in surrender to a life different than we expected, but somehow more than we imagined. We press into grief and processing; yet we press into joy and abundance, a life still worth living.

I recently re-read the first words in my journal after Winnie's death:

Give sorrow words;

the grief that does not speak

whispers the o'er-fraught heart

and bids it break.

-William Shakespeare, Macbeth[3]

I've chosen to give my sorrow words. They don't come easily. They're shared with intention and purpose. There is hope, but it's not all hope. There is space for lament: naming the wrongs, speaking the pain, sharing the burden.

I write, and share, and release. In these actions there is healing: healing from the messages that tell me it helped them feel less alone; healing from the burden carried by so many others; healing from the deep pain that longs to burrow and root and overgrow in my heart and soul.

May my words be His words, may my story reflect His Story, and may these words be a blessing to you. To Him be the glory for ever and ever. Amen.

And for us this the end of all the stories, and we can most truly say that they all lived happily ever after. But for them it was only the beginning of the real story. All their life in this world and all their adventures in Narnia had only been the cover and the title page: now at last they were beginning Chapter One of the Great Story which no one on earth has read: which goes on for ever: in which every chapter is better than the one before.

—*C. S. Lewis*

Be Thou My Vision

Dallan Forgaill

Eleanor H. Hull

Take My Life and Let It Be

Frances R. Havergal

H.A. Cesar Malan

Take my life__ and__ let it be   Con - se - crat - ed,__ Lord, to__ Thee;
Take my hands and__ let them move   At the im - pulse of Thy__ love;
Take my voice and__ let me sing   Al- ways, on - ly,__ for my__ King;
Take my sil - ver__ and my gold   Not a mite would I with-hold;
Take my will__ and__ make it Thine It shall be__ no long-er__ mine;
Take my love; my__ Lord, I pour   At Thy feet__ its__ trea sure__ store;

Take my mo - ments and my days,__   Let them flow in
Take my feet and__ let them be__   Swift and beau - ti -
Take my lips and__ let them be__   Filled with mes - sa -
Take my in - tel - lect and use__   Ev - 'ry pow'r as
Take my heart it__ is Thine own,__ It shall be Thy
Take my - self and__ I will be__   Ev - er, on - ly,

cease - less__ praise,__   Let them flow in__ cease - less praise.
ful__ for__ Thee,__   Swift and beau - ti - ful for Thee.
ges__ from__ Thee,__   Filled with mes - sa - ges from Thee.
Thou shalt__ choose,   Ev - 'ry pow'r as__ Thou shalt choose.
roy - al__ throne,__   It shall be Thy__ roy - al throne.
all__ for__ Thee,__   Ev - er, on - ly,__ all for Thee.

Acknowledgements

The biggest of heartfelt thanks:

To Sam for believing in me and holding me through it all. Thank you for letting me share our story with the world. Thank you for walking by my side and being my best friend.

To my family for loving and cheering me on. Especially to my parents, who bolstered my independence and gave me the example of a serving heart and a critical mind.

To friends and family (far and near) who have faithfully followed our story, our blog, my writing, and have championed this book into existence. To my friends who helped me with countless decisions and checked up on me these past few years.

To Allison Clouse, Kelley Mitchell, and Emily Chappell for reading my oh-so-rough first draft and still believing in me. Your encouragement carried me for months.

To Emily Chappell for being my book doula, workout buddy, writing coach, and editor. I couldn't have done it without you!

To my dear friend Tiffany Nardoni for going first in a great many things—marriage, parenthood, child loss, adoption, and writing a book. I have watched closely and gleaned much from your courageous journey.

For the countless people who watched a cute toddling girl named Corrie so I could write and edit, especially Grandma Pam and Grandpa Dave.

To HopeWriters for offering a community for budding authors. Finding this safe place to grow was critical to the birth of this book.

To countless authors who wrote the books I needed to read, especially C. S. Lewis, Corrie ten Boom, Timothy Keller, Nancy Guthrie, Sally Lloyd-Jones, Eugene Peterson, Tom Zuba, and Angie Smith, among many others. Your words are a gift to the world. Thank you for sharing.

To my Grieving Together mamas for listening to me, especially through the year after Clive died. The sisterhood found among our group is unmatched and

I'm forever grateful to have found you all.

To the bereaved mamas who came after me, especially Jenna, Hayley, and Sarah. While I wrote, I often thought of your grieving hearts and remembered Jamie, Monroe, and Aubrey.

To my precious Corrie for the smiles and laughs you give me daily. May you know the great joy you bring me, and may you be confident in your pursuits. May you always be hidden under His wings and know where your home is. You are a treasure.

To baby-on-the-way Miles for your kicking reminders of the duty of delight. You are so loved and wanted. We expectantly wait for you and trust the mystery unfolding before us. God is mighty.

To Clive for giving me such an example of courage, strength, and joy. I never knew such a small boy would make such an impact. You are still treasured and loved. You are so missed. He has called you by name, you are His.

To my wildflower, Winnie, for your graceful peace. As you fill my heart with love, you make me long for restoration. I'm reminded of your beauty in the beauty surrounding me, and I'll always carry you with me. You are fearfully and wonderfully made, my sweet daughter.

To my God who sat with me and walked with me, allowing me to question, doubt, and lament. My journey is still unfolding. Thank you for your patience with me as your child. Also, thank you for creating a glorious thing called coffee.

Notes

Chapter 1: Lament

p. 7   1 Lewis, C. S. *The Problem of Pain.* HarperCollins, 2002, p. 9.

p. 14   2 Brueggemann, Walter. *Spirituality of the Psalms.* Fortress Press, 2001.

p. 16   3 Shakespeare, William. *Macbeth.* Dover Publications, 1993, IV.3.245.

p. 19   4 Matheson, George. "O Love that Wilt Not Let Me Go." Composed by Albert Peace. Public Domain, 1882. michaelkravchuk.com/free-choir-sheet-music-o-love-that-wilt-not-let-me-go.

p. 22   5 Mathis, David. "Here I Raise My Ebenezer." *Desiring God,* 7 Feb. 2019, www.desiringgod.org/articles/here-i-raise-my-ebenezer.

Chapter 2: Peace

p. 25   1 Lewis, C. S. *Mere Christianity.* HarperCollins, 2008, p. 50.

p. 31   2 Butts, Mary. *Fence of Trust.* United Society of Christian Endeavors, 1898, p. 7.

p. 37   3 Mote, Edward. "My Hope is Built on Nothing Less." Composed by John Bacchus Dykes. Public Domain, 1834. michaelkravchuk.com/free-choir-sheet-music-my-hope-is-built-on-nothing-less.

p. 38   4 Lewis, C. S. *Mere Christianity.* HarperCollins, 2008, p. 32.

p. 42   5 This concept was from our Griefshare Workbook. We recommend finding a support group near you at griefshare.org

Chapter 3: Comfort

p. 47   1 Lewis, C. S. *Yours, Jack: Spiritual Direction from C.S. Lewis.* Edited by Paul F. Ford, HarperCollins, 2008, p. 326.

p. 58   2 For more thoughts and a study on the book of Job as it relates to grief, read: Guthrie, Nancy. *Holding Onto Hope.* Tyndale, 2015.

p. 65   3 Lemmel, Helen H. "Turn Your Eyes Upon Jesus." Public Domain, 1918. michaelkravchuk.com/free-choir-sheet-music-turn-your-eyes-upon-jesus.

Chapter 4: Love

p. 74   1 Hurnard, Hannah. *Hinds Feet on High Places.* Wilder Publications, 2010, p. 40.

p. 74   2 For references to these name changes, see the following scriptures: Ruth 1, Genesis 17, Act 13, Genesis 32, and John 1.

p. 75   3 Lewis, C. S. *Mere Christianity.* HarperCollins, 2008, p. 226.

p. 79   4 Lewis, C. S. *A Grief Observed.* HarperCollins, 2001, p. 11.

p. 81   5 Baldwin, James. *The Fire Next Time.* Penguin Books, 2017.

p. 83　6 "What Wondrous Love is This." American Spiritual. Arranged by Michael Kravchuk. Public Domain, 1811. michaelkravchuk.com/free-choir-sheet-music-what-wondrous-love-is-this

p. 84　7 Mote, Edward. "My Hope is Built on Nothing Less." Composed by John Bacchus Dykes. Public Domain, 1834. michaelkravchuk.com/free-choir-sheet-music-my-hope-is-built-on-nothing-less.

p. 87　8 Ussishkin, David. "On Nehemiah's City Wall and the Size of Jerusalem during the Persian Period." *New Perspectives on Ezra-Nehemiah: History and Historiography, Text, Literature, and Interpretation*, by Isaac Kalimi, Eisenbrauns, 2012, pp. 101–130.

Chapter 5: Faith

p. 95　1 Lewis, C. S. *Till We Have Faces: A Myth Retold*. Houghton Mifflin Harcourt, 2012, p. 308.

p. 99　2 For more thoughts on walking in relationship with God, read: Jethani, Skye. *With: Reimagining the Way You Relate to God*. Thomas Nelson Publishers, 2011.

p. 104　3 For more thoughts on practicing Silence and Solitude, read: Barton, Ruth Haley. *Invitation to Solitude and Silence*. InterVarsity Press, 2010.

p. 105　4 Saint Augustine of Hippo, *Sermons* 4.1.1

p. 111　5 Chisholm, Thomas. "Great Is Thy Faithfulness." Composed by William Runyan. Public Domain, 1923. michaelkravchuk.com/free-choir-sheet-music-great-is-thy-faithfulness.

Chapter 6: Hope

p. 119　1 Lewis, C. S. *Yours, Jack: Spiritual Direction from C.S. Lewis*. Edited by Paul F. Ford, HarperCollins, 2008, p. 369.

p. 120　2 "Family Tragedy." *The American Colony in Jerusalem*, Library of Congress, 2005, www.loc.gov/exhibits/americancolony/amcolony-family.html.

p. 120　3 Simmermacher, Gunther. "Biography of Hymns: It Is Well With My Soul." *The Southern Cross*, 14 July 2014, www.scross.co.za/2014/07/hymns-it-is-well/.

p. 126　4 Dickinson, Emily. *Selected Poems and Letters of Emily Dickinson*. Edited by Robert N. Linscott, Doubleday, 1959, p. 79.

p. 128　5 Lewis, C. S. *Mere Christianity*. HarperCollins, 2008, p. 226.

p. 131　6 Spafford, Horatio. "It Is Well With My Soul." Composed by Phillip Bliss. Public Domain, 1876. michaelkravchuk.com/free-choir-sheet-music-it-is-well-with-my-soul.

Chapter 7: Grace

p. 139　1 Lewis, C. S. *Yours, Jack: Spiritual Direction from C.S. Lewis*. Edited by Paul F. Ford, HarperCollins, 2008, p. 144.

p. 140　2 Lewis, C. S. *A Grief Observed*. HarperCollins, 2001, p. 10.

p. 141　3 Ten Boom, Corrie, and Jamie Buckingham. *Tramp for the Lord*. Revell, 1974, p. 183.

p. 149   4 Ten Boom, Corrie, John Sherrill, and Elizabeth Sherrill. *The Hiding Place*. Chosen Books, 1971, p. 195-197.

p. 149   5 Ten Boom, Corrie. "Guideposts Classics: Corrie ten Boom on Forgiveness." *Guideposts*, November 1972. https://guideposts.org/better-living/positive-living/guideposts-classics-corrie-ten-boom-on-forgiveness.

p. 151   6 Robinson, Robert. "Come Thou Fount of Every Blessing." Public Domain, 1758. michaelkravchuk.com/free-sheet-music-for-choir-come-thou-fount-of-every-blessing.

p. 155   7 Ten Boom, Corrie, and Jamie Buckingham. *Tramp for the Lord*. Revell, 1974, p. 55.

Chapter 8: Courage

p. 163   2 Lewis, C. S. *A Grief Observed*. HarperCollins, 2001, p. 3.

p. 162   1 As quoted in Cooper, Gustafson, and Salah. *Becoming a Great School*. Rowman & Littlefield, 2013, p. ix.

p. 166   3 As quoted in: Valcárcel, Dorothy. "Transformation Garden." *Crosswalk* , 17 May 2010, www.crosswalk.com/devotionals/transformgarden/transformation-garden-may-17-2010-11631709.html.

p. 168   4 Blakemore, Erin. "Mary Todd Lincoln Became a Laughingstock After Her Husband's Assassination." *History.com*, A&E Television Networks, 13 Apr. 2018, www.history.com/news/mary-todd-lincoln-assassination-facts.

p. 168   5 Golding , Connie. "The Lincoln Family Line: A Tragic Legacy ." *Ford's Theatre*, 2015, www.fords.org/blog/post/the-lincoln-family-line-a-tragic-legacy.

p. 178   6 Schaff, Philip. *Christ in Song*. New York, Anson D. F. Randolph & Company, 1869, p 521.

p. 183   7 Luther, Martin. "A Mighty Fortress Is Our God." Public Domain, c. 1529. michaelkravchuk.com/free-choir-sheet-music-a-mighty-fortress-is-our-god.

Chapter 9: Joy

p. 188   1 Julian of Norwich. *Revelations of Divine Love*. Oxford University Press, 2015.

p. 190   2 C. S. Lewis, *The Great Divorce*. HarperOne, 2015.

p. 192   3 Vanauken, Sheldon. *A Severe Mercy*. Harper & Row, 1977.

p. 196   4 Williams, Margery. *The Velveteen Rabbit*. Delacorte Press, 1991, pp. 5-6.

p. 197   5 Frankl, Viktor E. *Man's Search for Meaning*. Beacon Press, 2014.

p. 200   6 Lewis, C. S. *Mere Christianity*. HarperCollins, 2008, p. 226.

p. 202   7 Voskamp, Ann. *One Thousand Gifts*. Zondervan, 2010.

p. 203   8 Van Dyke, Henry. "Joyful, Joyful, We Adore Thee." Public Domain, 1907. michaelkravchuk.com/free-choir-sheet-music-joyful-joyful-we-adore-thee.

Chapter 10: Your Story

p. 211   1 Lewis, C. S. *Yours, Jack: Spiritual Direction from C.S. Lewis.* Edited by Paul F. Ford, HarperCollins, 2008, p. 326.

p. 215   2 Manning, Brennan. *Abba's Child: The Cry of the Heart for Intimate Belonging.* NavPress, 2015.

p. 217   3 Some of these concepts were gathered from the following resources:

Le Rucher Ministries debriefing retreat materials, lerucher.org.

Allen, Jennie. *Chase Study.* Thomas Nelson, 2012.

Ross, Melody. *Soul Restoration Workbook.* Brave Girls Club, 2016.

p. 219   4 Crosby, Fanny. "Blessed Assurance." Composed by Phoebe P. Knapp. Public Domain, 1873. michaelkravchuk.com/free-sheet-music-for-choir-blessed-assurance

Chapter 11: Our Story

p. 222   1 Lewis, C. S. *A Grief Observed.* HarperCollins, 2001, p. 59.

p. 235   2 Ten Boom, Corrie, John Sherrill, and Elizabeth Sherrill. *The Hiding Place.* Chosen Books, 1971.

p. 240   3 Shakespeare, William. *Macbeth.* Dover Publications, 1993, IV.3.245.

p. 241   4 Lewis, C. S. *The Last Battle.* HarperCollins, 2002.

p. 242   5 Forgaill, Dallan. "Be Thou My Vision." Arranged by Eleanor H. Hull. Public Domain, c. 6th Century. michaelkravchuk.com/free-choir-sheet-music-be-thou-my-vision.

p. 243   6 Havergal, Frances. "Take My Life and Let It Be." Composed by H.A. Cesar Malan. Public Domain, 1874. michaelkravchuk.com/free-choir-sheet-music-take-my-life-and-let-it-be.

Further Reading

Chapter 1: Lament
No More Faking Fine - Esther Fleece
Permission to Mourn - Tom Zuba

Chapter 2: Peace
Boundaries - Henry Cloud and John Townsend

Chapter 3: Comfort
Holding onto Hope - Nancy Guthrie
I Will Carry You - Angie Smith

Chapter 4: Love
Hinds Feet on High Places - Hannah Hurnard

Chapter 5: Faith
With: Reimagining the Way You Relate to God - Skye Jethani
Invitation to Solitude and Silence - Ruth Haley Barton
When God Doesn't Fix It - Laura Story
Walking with God Through Pain and Suffering - Timothy Keller

Chapter 6: Hope
Safe in the Arms of God - John MacArthur

Chapter 7: Grace
The Hiding Place - Corrie ten Boom
Tramp for the Lord - Corrie ten Boom

Chapter 8: Courage
The Heavenly Man - Brother Yun
The Screwtape Letters - C. S. Lewis

Chapter 9: Joy
One Thousand Gifts - Ann Voskamp
A Severe Mercy - Sheldon Vanauken
Man's Search for Meaning - Viktor Frankl

Chapter 10: Your Story
A Grief Observed - C. S. Lewis
Still - Tiffany Nardoni
Even Broken Can Be Beautiful - Sarah Rieke

Music for the Grieving Heart

I've compiled some favorite songs and created a playlist for each chapter.
You can find the playlists at samandrachelgeorge.com/music or by searching
#grievecreatebelieve on Spotify.

Stay in Touch

Thank you for reading my story. I'd love to hear from you and stay in touch.
You can find me at:

Instagram: @rachelgeorgewrites

Facebook.com/rachelgeorgewrites

Blog and resources: samandrachelgeorge.com

Share on social media with #grievecreatebelieve

If you're willing, I'd love to have you review my book on Amazon and to share about it with friends or family who would appreciate it. Thank you for supporting independent authors like myself!

Made in the USA
Coppell, TX
06 February 2021